LAYMAN'S LIBRARY OF CHRISTIAN DOCTRINE

The Mission of the Church

JESSE C. FLETCHER

BROADMAN PRESS
Nashville, Tennessee

4216-44

ISBN: 0-8054-1644-7

Dewey Decimal Classification: 262

Subject Headings: CHURCH

Library of Congress Catalog Card Number: 87-20959

Printed in the United States of America

Library of Congress Cataloging-in-Publication Data

Fletcher, Jesse C.
  Mission of the church.

  (Layman's library of Christian doctrine ; 14)
  Bibliography: p.
  Includes index.
  1. Mission of the church.   I. Title.   II. Series.
BV601.8.F57   1988   266'.001   87-20959
ISBN 0-8054-1644-7

Foreword

The *Layman's Library of Christian Doctrine* in sixteen volumes covers the major doctrines of the Christian faith.

To meet the needs of the lay reader, the *Library* is written in a popular style. Headings are used in each volume to help the reader understand which part of the doctrine is being dealt with. Technical terms, if necessary to the discussion, will be clearly defined.

The need for this series is evident. Christians need to have a theology of their own, not one handed to them by someone else. The *Library* is written to help readers evaluate and form their own beliefs based on the Bible and on clear and persuasive statements of historic Christian positions. The aim of the series is to help laymen hammer out their own personal theology.

The books range in size from 140 pages to 168 pages. Each volume deals with a major part of Christian doctrine. Although some overlap is unavoidable, each volume will stand on its own. A set of the sixteen-volume series will give a person a complete look at the major doctrines of the Christian church.

Each volume is personalized by its author. The author will show the vitality of Christian doctrines and their meaning for everyday life. Strong and fresh illustrations will hold the interest of the reader. At times the personal faith of the authors will be seen in illustrations from their own Christian pilgrimage.

Not all laymen are aware they are theologians. Many may believe they know nothing of theology. However, every person believes something. This series helps the layman to understand what he believes and to be able to be "prepared to make a defense to anyone who calls him to account for the hope that is in him" (1 Pet. 3:15, RSV).

Contents

Introduction

The church plays a pivotal role in the study of Christian doctrine. The *Layman's Library of Christian Doctrine* dedicated three of its sixteen volumes to exploring different parts of the church's role. *The Nature of the Church,* volume 12, and *The Life of the Church,* volume 13, are helpful but not necessary introductions to this volume, *The Mission of the Church.*

The Nature of the Church is much more intent on developing what theologians call an ecclesiology or doctrine of the church than it is in focusing on either the church's life or its mission. No doctrine of the church, however, is complete unless it takes seriously the ongoing life of the church as a continuing incarnation of Christ and the ongoing mission of the church as its fundamental calling.

In the same way, *The Life of the Church,* which focuses on the church as a caring, worshiping, and serving community, lays groundwork to move to the mission of the church.

The need for this volume should be apparent, with its first chapter, "The Church of the Mission." The mission is not first the church's; it is God's, and the church is the result of God's mission. But the church born of that mission quickly discovers that it in turn exists for mission. Perhaps no more famous quotation on the subject can be found than Emil

7

Brunner's, "The church exists by mission as a fire exists by burning."[1]

Of course, the analogy can lead to some ridiculous questions. Does a fire need to know it is burning to know that it is a fire? Does a church need to know that it is in mission to know that it is a church? Ironically the answer may be yes.

For the church not to know that it exists by mission leaves it in danger of spending its days without the sense of purpose which explains its nature and its life. The very existence of the church, the structure of the church, and the gifts with which the church ministers have their meaning only when the church senses its calling, that is, its mission.

In this sense the individual Christian's experience serves as an analogy for the church. Christians experience the love of God in Christ and a sense of forgiveness and wholeness that comes with the new birth that issues from the act of faith. For Christians to try to live life without understanding that it has a unique purpose in God's plan is tragic.

I made the personal commitment called "receiving Christ" as a preteen. But growth was slow, and adolescence often seemed to be unaffected by that experience. Yet, as a young man, I was confronted with a strong sense of God's purpose for my life and my Christian experience came alive. I discovered that God had gifted me for tasks which He would reveal to me as time went on. That discovery became exciting and galvanizing and growth producing. I scrambled to prepare myself as I had not been willing to before. I was ready to discipline myself in a way that I could not motivate myself to do before. Each day jumped with the excitement, and the future stretched like a beckoning horizon before me. I had a "vocation," in the classical sense of the word, a calling.

This sense of God's calling is equally important to the church, the body of Christ, the church that Jesus spoke of when He said "I will build my church" (Matt. 16:18). This is the church that encompasses believers throughout history and everywhere in any given time frame by whatever name they might identify themselves or in whatever fellowship they might gather.

The church is also to be understood as a local and gathered fellowship. There its leadership is obvious, its gifts are incarnate in the life of its members, and its days are being lived out in witness to Jesus Christ and in the mission to which He has called it. In fact, in the New Testament reference to the local church is made far more than to the universal body of Christ. All doctrinal talk about the mission of the church has to be translated into the language of a local church in mission for it to have effective meaning.

But it is important that the reader understand that this volume addresses the church in its broadest sense in order to profit the church in its most localized sense. The context will make it obvious to which sense I am referring. I sincerely hope that the reader, most likely a believer, will sense an identification with the church in its broadest sense, historically and geographically, without hangups about denominational or doctrinal distinctives. Such distinctives have shaped and will continue to shape the church's expression of its mission. Some of the existing differences will be discussed shortly because they are revelant, but they do not stand in the way of the mission of the church. Its mission transcends such differences and informs and constrains any church as it tries to understand its own life and set its own agenda for mission.

A few years ago an unlikely outbreak of Christian life emerged among a tribe of people on the coast of the Indian Ocean in East Africa. The Giryama Tribe exploded with Christian life following the witness of a small group of missionaries and national Christians in one of their villages. The good news in Jesus Christ was so exciting to each who heard it that he or she in turn rushed to share with family members, neighbors, and friends. There were almost no barriers to acceptance, and churches sprang up in villages faster than the missionaries or the more mature Christians could find them or follow through.

The more mature Christians had their work cut out for them in the disciplining and directing process. One of them confessed the pure pleasure involved in such a witness. He explained that there was no denominational question to resolve, no minute differences to explain, no historical developments to clarify, no "theological turf" to defend. It was simply a matter of watching the gospel ignite in a heart and burn so ferociously that it began to consume all the hearts around it.

Over 150 churches were founded as 2,000 people received baptism. The excitement of the new life of this people was such that they hungered for the Word, for its promise and power with no need to structure it in theologies or debate possible interpretations.

One of the burdens that the individual Christian and the church as a whole must bear is that new Christians experiencing such pure joy of their "Eden" must face the more difficult realities of informed Christian existence. But such joy does speak to something that no church or believer must ever lose sight of: The gospel transcends differences, and the mission of the church in its purest sense does not recognize them.

Of course, an alert reader may quickly sense the irony of such sentiments. For instance, they are being expressed in one volume of a multivolume approach to Christian doctrine. Isn't this just one more writer attempting to explain mission so that the church can understand more clearly the great and complex theological atmosphere in which it exist? That is a difficult question to escape. As the individual believer ponders his own reality, all that God is about, and the reality of the church, he is involved in structuring his understanding in theologies.

The thrust of this volume is that mission must be seen as transcending theological formulation. It must be understood as inherent in both the nature and the life of the church. Perhaps at this point Francis DuBose's statement can help us: "Mission does not so much need to be justified theologically as theology needs to be understood missiologically."[2] In other words, in the very midst of understanding Christian doctrine, in purposeful and sincere theologizing, the believer and the church desperately need to understand its mission not as a very small part but as the core of it all.

Yet Arthur Glasser pointed out that understanding the mission of the church is more complicated than that. He said:

> Never before have so many missions and missionaries been so fruitfully engaged in making Christ known. On the other hand, never has the church had to cope with so many articulate voices advancing theologies of mission, not only hostile to this activity but challenging its very validly.[3]

In fact, Arthur Glasser and Donald McGavaran have spent quite sometime identifying the major approaches to mission taken by the modern church. The implication of their analysis, of course, is that there is a "right way" or at least a "better way."

According to Glasser and moving from left to right in a political and theological sense, ideas about mission include the liberation theology concept the conciliar theology of mission (taking its name from the World Council of Churches), the Roman Catholic view, and the Contemporary Evangelical view. Most of their distinctions revolve around evangelism.[4]

Francis DuBose expressed some strong questions about the direction of discussions over evangelism when he said:

> We rightly decry what has happened to evangelism in this century, but the manipulative (imperalistic) and selective (racist) evangelism of the extreme right has been just as unbiblical as the insipid and anemic evangelism (nonevangelism) of the extreme left. The way to return to biblical evangelism is not to deny to mission the validity of ministry and service when the New Testament so clearly and definitively includes it.[5]

My personal conviction is that a rediscovery of the mission of the church is the way up from a temporary scene preoccupied with divisions caused by empty rhetoric, wasted resources, lack of focus and milling lives not yet aware of the unique challenge God has set before us. But the point of view in this book recognizes that there is room for fellowships of varying kinds with different concerns and making different emphases.

Glasser and McGavran recognized this when they said:

> Mission is a vast enterprise made up of many kinds of missions, many kinds of activities, carried on cross-culturally by many kinds of Christians. A great diversity in motives had led to many kinds of mission.[6]

In other words, groups of believers, understanding themselves as church, must grasp the transcendent need to be about mission with as little lost motion as possible from infighting on how or where, or even why.

If a compelling mission of the church is rediscovered, it is sure to revitalize the church wherever it happens and to bear fruit on a broad spectrum of fronts impacted by that church. While this volume often focuses on understanding, it is also intended to provoke agenda making and, more importantly, action.

Perhaps an overview of what this book will cover is in order. "The Church of the Mission," Chapter 1, affirms the initial and essential truths that recognize that it is first God's mission. The church is His creation in Christ sustained and nurtured by His spirit and called to enter into the mission He brought into being. The church must understand that its mission is derived from God's mission.

The second chapter reviews the church's biblical commission. It attempts to look at mission in terms of its Old Testament heritage, its New Testament mandates, and its implications for both individual believers and churches. This section introduces the impact of the ongoing model for mission found in the life and ministry of Jesus Christ.

The third chapter examines the march of missions through time and space as well as through political and denominational structures. This approach resists the temptation of a thoroughgoing history of missions or a detailed analysis of its geographical spread in favor of a simple summary. That the church of the mission has to grapple with political realities that have been geographically and culturally shaped goes without saying. It is an effort to enhance an understanding of mission in terms of church and denominational growth and expansion.

The fourth chapter analyzes the territory covered in the previous chapter in terms of the message of mission. Different emphases in different periods give the impression of change. Has the mission changed? Or is there an abiding core?

The fifth chapter lays a groundwork for agenda making and approaches methods of missions in a nontraditional way. Bypassing the traditional evangelistic, educational, and medical divisions, the methods of mission are seen as incarnational, demographical, territorial, and connectional. The incarnational umbrella builds on the model that Jesus Christ brings to mission methods in terms of preaching, teaching, and response to human need. When David Livingstone hacked his way through the jungles of West Africa toward the great plateaus of its central regions, he was laying groundwork for territorial expansion as well as driving a stake in the heart of the slave trade.

But those who study the church's mission (missiologists) have recognized that mission is a uniquely demographical enterprise. In other words, it reaches people in terms of racial, cultural, and language groups even more than in territorial concentrations. Many dedicated efforts have developed around such demographic realities.

The Wycliffe Translators have long distinquished themselves in mission heroics by identifying language groups without access to the Scriptures and paying a great price, often in out-of-the-way and dangerous environments, to reduce a language of a people, sometimes less than a hundred in number, to Scriptures. That illustrates another aspect of the methods of mission: its connectional needs.

Traditionally modern mission connectional methods have been divided between societies, denominations, and independent boards. The fundamental connection, of course, is the church. Therefore, the mission of the church is critical to the way the church does its work.

This volume is not meant to argue the pros and cons of various connectional approaches but only to point out that connectionalism is an inevitable outgrowth of a sense of mission. Some connection is inherent in the nature of the task.

Since the local church is the basic Christian connection, the focus turns to the mission of a local church. I hope the reader can begin translating the history and principles of the previous chapter summaries into a local focus in Chapter 6.

Chapter 7 turns to the current scene. Mission occurs in the meantime: It is happening in the time between the coming of Christ, which brought the church into being, and the return of Christ, which will consummate the mission He began. Meantime urgency has historically motivated believers and churches in mission. It has caused them to undergo incredible meantime difficulties in its task.

In the upper reaches of the Northwestern United States, the indomitable salmon undergo a most arduous journey every year to its spawning grounds. Many perish in the process, but they have no choice but to undertake the journey; it is built into them. Christians have the need for mission built into their spiritual life but do not often follow through. God has allowed His children a right of choice that He has not allowed His other creatures. However, when Christians discover mission, they often experience an inner compulsion and undertake tremendous hardships to do what God has planted in their hearts to do.

Christians on mission continue to face difficulties. Some are obvious and historic. Others are more subtle. A straightforward look at mean-time intimidations is included in Chapter 7.

But no consideration of the mission of the church today would be complete without drawing encouragement from the mean-time victories being recorded around the world in a variety of mission activities and among all kinds of people.

If this volume serves the purpose for which it was written, it will lead the believer to be a part of the church's effort to embrace anew its mission, make agenda for the task, and review its activities and resources and gifts. It will help a church set honest priorities that will guide it in the expenditures of its energy and in the living of its days.

Nothing is more tragic than to scan church history and encounter the church without vision. In the same context nothing is more exciting than when the church discovers and embraces its mission. I hope that is happening to the church now because it's obvious that mission is in transition and that the church is again at the crossroads.

Notes

1. Emil Brunner, *The Word in the World,* p. 108.
2. Francis M. Dubose, *God Who Sends,* p. 149.
3. Arthur F. Glasser and Donald A. McGavran, *Contemporary Theologies of Mission,* p. 7.
4. Ibid.
5. Dubose, pp. 123, 125.
6. Glasser and McGavran, p. 16.

1

The Church of the Mission

To understand the mission of the church one must first come to understand the church of the mission. The church is the result of what the theologians call the *missio dei,* the mission of God. God's mission to the world, that in Christ He declared that He loved (John 3:16), resulted in the church. But the church is not the end of mission. It is an instrument of God's hands to accomplish the next part of His mission. The church's mission emerges from God's mission.

Arising from the Nature of God

For many people the mission of the church begins with the Great Commission. This is like saying a great highway begins at an important junction somewhere along the way. The mission of the church begins with the nature of God. Christians should center their mission around the God who called them out and called the church into being. God calls us to center ourselves in Himself.

Creation

Jesus revealed that God truly loved the world. But revelation in the time before Christ had testified that God was this world's Creator and that man was God's growing creation. His loving activity in the voids of space brought into being our world and, ultimately, the humanity that we are and that we so desperately try to understand as we probe our origins. We are God's creation, and Christ says God loves us.

We can better understand who we are today if we look about us and see God's creative hand. The persons walking in and out of our lives are part of this creation, just as we are. The ground on which we stand and which brings forth the bounty that sustains us is from God's hand. The atmosphere in which we live and breathe, the weather patterns that swirl around us, the ecology which we treat so carelessly, even ruthlessly, is a part of His loving creation.

Years ago a renowned musician and scholar named Albert Schweitzer became so convinced of God's love that he turned from a career in philosophy and music to become a medical doctor. He spent the rest of his days in the steamy jungles of West Africa, trying to live out God's love in healing mercies.

The trait that characterized Schweitzer's life even more than his personal sacrifice was his reverence for life. He carried this reverence to a point that some felt was ridiculous. He refused to step on the tiniest creature, and he took no life that could be avoided. He became a vegetarian.

Anytime he put his hand to another human being or another life form, anytime he moved through the environment in which he lived, anytime he looked up at the sky and into the vastness of space it was with a reverance for life. Schweitzer understood that his mission arose from the nature of the creative God, and he reverenced the creation that issued from God's hand.

Paul said that the whole creation groans in travail, awaiting redemption by its Creator. The devastating hand of sin puts every aspect of this creation in jeopardy; only the loving, patient activity of the Creator gives promise of total redemption.

Redemptive Purpose

The God of creation who set humankind as the epitome of His creation with the power to accept or reject Him, to obey Him or disobey, to come to Him or go from Him, could have recoiled in agony and disgust when the fatal manifestation of sin became so clear. The cancer was not just in human hearts, the whole environment reflected it. The story of God's activity in history since then, however, reveals just the opposite response. God loved His creation even more. Like a human father who will not give up on the most wayward son (the story that Jesus told so powerfully in trying to describe God's love), the heavenly Father reached out.

God's grand purpose embraced all nations, all humanity. It arches through all time and encompasses all peoples in all places. And it will triumph because it emerges from the very heart of the Creator, God.

God's Character

In *Understanding Christian Missions,* Herbert Kane developed the missionary mandate in a discussion that begins with the character of God. Kane believed God's character can be described in terms of attributes, such as His eternal being, His personal nature, His infinite dimensions, His morality, His Trinity, and His self-revelation. But the two characteristics that reflect directly His purposes for the world, and ultimately His mission, are revealed in 1 John as light and love.[1]

Light spells out splendor, glory, truth, and holiness. God's purity emerges in the light. Sin's hand brought a darkness upon creation and into the heart of humankind. God's light reaches into the darkness with the power to dissipate it. His light reveals His mission.

But we begin to experience His true nature toward us in His love. In fact, the Scripture says that God is love (1 John 4:16). It was not that we loved God but that God loved us that brought about the great redemptive effort.

Redemptive Action

The God of light and love purposed to redeem mankind. He began by raising up a people whom He uniquely enlisted to accomplish His task. The Bible reveals God as a covenant God. He covenanted with Abraham to bless all nations and all people through his descendants. The Great Commission encompasses all nations, but the root of that promise goes all the way back to Genesis.

Through Abraham God raised up a people, Israel, and set them on mission. Israel was the nation of the mission before the church was the church of the mission. Israel was to bring forth the Messiah. God did not intend just to select the best and brightest from His creation, as He had chosen Saul to lead Israel. The mission was too demanding, too awesome, too hard, involved too much suffering, and had consquences eternal in nature. God sent His Son for that task. Just as he had provided Abraham with the sacrificial lamb, so He provided Israel with the Suffering Savior.

The mission of the church arises from the mission of God. God is the Sender, and He sent His Son.

Arising from the Nature of the Son

The church of the mission arises from the nature of the Son. This is obvious because the work of Christ brought the church into being. It is profound because the church continues to be Christ in the world.

The church is the body given to Christ, the conquering Savior. Howard Snyder said:

God has chosen to place the church with Christ at the very center of His plan to reconcile the world to Himself. The church's mission, therefore, is to glorify God by continuing in the world the works of the kingdom which Jesus began.[2]

But that is like beginning at the end. The beginning is Christ because He was at the beginning (John 1:1). His incarnate and mysterious life begins to explain the church.

The Kingdom of God

Jesus Christ announced the kingdom of God and gave the church a theme as well as a gospel. The kingdom of God is the rule of God in people's hearts. It is eternal. It was here with Christ just as He was here. As the church reflects Christ's continuing presence, the kingdom of God is here. God's kingdom is not established in external forms but is hidden in the hearts of people and is manifested in their obedience to the Heavenly Father. But, more, Christ made possible life in the kingdom by dealing with the sin that separates us and the death that threatens us. Jesus' voluntary sacrifice on the cross dramatized God's great reconciling love for us. His resurrection from the dead announced His dominion over death. As the risen Lord, He called the apostles and the church to proclaim to the world the good news of redemption and the kingdom of God in which the redeemed lived.

Enabling Spirit

The Son continues His work by enabling the church through His continuing presence in the Spirit. The gift of the Holy Spirit enabled the apostle in the community of faith to witness. "The Holy Ghost continues the mission which God has begun in His Son Jesus Christ until Jesus Himself will return and terminate the mission."[3]

Jesus said that as the Father sent Him so He would send His followers (John 20:21). The church has a mission precisely because it is an extension of God's mission in Jesus Christ.

Jesus called the church forth to this task with words like *come, follow,* and *go.* Christ's invitation, "Come to me" (Matt. 11:28), is not only the basis for the church being called forth to Himself but also unto His mission. In turn Christ called those who "come" to "follow." "If any man would come after me, let him deny himself and take up his cross and follow me" (Matt. 16:24).

Since Christ is on mission, surely the church of that mission should be following Him. His Spirit leads and shows the church what to do daily. The whole concept of growth or being "disciples" emerges from following after Him.

The church of the mission is the church in training for that mission. Christ's life and teaching constitute the curriculum. The spiritual dynamic is found in "following Christ." Believers who make up the church develop the Christlike spirit when they have a sense of following the Son and learning from Him.

In recent years an elderly Roman Catholic nun known as Mother Teresa has gained quite a bit of notoriety in her work among the poor and homeless in India. Amid a deepening consciousness of hunger and suffering in the world, people respond to a Christlike spirit where they find it. Missions (all the church does in its mission) is best characterized by acts that reflect the spirit of Christ. This is not surprising since the church's mission arises from the nature of the Son.

In the modern missionary era, the apostle Paul is seen as the consummate missionary. He saw all missionary activity as arising from the Son and said, "For to me to live is Christ" (Phil. 1:21).

The mission is Christ's and the church is the body given

to Him to continue the task. Because the Sender sent Him and He sends the church, the church will always find its inspiration and direction in His example, His Spirit. His confidence, and His single-minded commitment to that which His Father had sent Him to do. The church can do no less than its Master.

Apostleship

Going transforms a disciple into an apostle. It literally means "sent one." Jesus was the chief apostle. Our apostleship comes from Him. The concept of an apostle looks to the church of the mission as it arises from the nature of the Father and from the nature of the Son.

This going develops its impetus in Jesus Christ. Christ's startling message that the kingdom of God is now present in our lives plus the good news that He has made it possible to be shared with men and women throughout the world results in going. But He was more specific.

Christ's last words were, "Go ye therefore" (Matt. 28:19, KJV). One must *come* to Christ before one can *follow* and one must *learn to follow* before one can *go,* but *go* one must to be obedient to Christ's full example. The church of the mission was now faced with the mission of the church.

Doing the Mission of the Church

For centuries believers have gone forth to share Christ and announce the kingdom of God. When their efforts result in establishing new congregations those churches can be understood as result. Because they are the result of God's mission in the world and because they are the result of Christ's sacrifice and triumphant victory over death, churches can be seen as the end of the process. Christ's own words, "I will build my church and the gates of hell shall not prevail against it" (Matt. 16:18, KJV), have such an irresistible ring. The church can seem to be the goal of all that is done as mission. The truth, however, is just the opposite. The church has become God's instrument for His mission. The church is sent to do the will of God even as Christ was sent to do God's will. The church is to announce the kingdom of God even as Jesus did. The church is to bring about God's grand design through living out its days and giving itself in obedience to Christ who is its head. The church is now on mission as well as the result of mission.

The church came into being as cause and effect. In a sense, the full circle of God's activity can be seen here. He chose a man, Abraham, to bring a people into being in covenant task. The people were given a man, the Messiah, God's own Son out of their midst that He might bring a new kind of covenant community, the church, into being for His task. Each individual in that covenant community becomes Abraham-like in his sentness and obedience. He becomes Christlike in that through faith he is in Christ and Christ is in him. That new covenant community, the church, is the body of Christ in Christ's continuing mission.

God's purpose of the ages which He has made know in Jesus Christ (Eph. 3:11) is now in the church's hands. The church is continually energized by the Father and the Son through the Holy Spirit. The mission of the church continues to be to glorify God by lifting up Christ to persons everywhere. The church's mission is the mission of Christ. Thus the mission of the church is to make Jesus Christ known to the world and to continue the mission that Jesus Himself set in motion through His cross. Simply, it is God's mission entrusted to His Son and passed on to His church.

From the beginning, God's redemptive activity in history seems invariably to be expressed through persons and a people. Today persons are the followers of Jesus Christ and the people is the church and the mission of the church is to glorify God through Christ. But the average believer and the average church often fail to sense their unique role in this broader biblical and historical definition of mission. They fail to realize that *missions* is doing *the mission* of the church. The church's ongoing life is many things, but its purpose is mission.

Hugo H. Culpepper correctly pointed out three problems the local church can encounter which can make its mission efforts less than healthy. The church can make mission less than its reason for being both as individual disciples of Christ and the church. It can do missions with unworthy motives and mistaken goals or objectives. It can fall into a spirit of arrogant pride in the task.[4]

If a local church allows missions to be one part or compartment of its life instead of galvanizing its whole, it misses the point. It is simply tipping its hat toward the task. An individual who does not understand life in Christ, the gifts of the Spirit, and personal opportunities as related to God's purpose through Christ in the church has not grasped the grand design. Many church members have protested mission projects by saying, "We pay missionaries to do that." Nothing could illustrate this tragic problem more clearly.

Equally important, missions must be done in the spirit of Christ and not for peer group approval or personal greatness or the accumulation of power. The individual believer's reward and the local church's reward are the same—the sense of well-being in living out the life of Christ in response to a world composed of individuals in great need of His good news and its healing hope.

To have a healthy sense of mission, the church should not fall into arrogant pride. Mission is not just church extension. As missiologist Lesslie Newbigin pointed out in his book *The Open Secret: Sketches for a Missionary Theology:*

> Mission is not essentially an action by which the church puts forth its own power and wisdom to conquer the world around it; it is, rather, an action of God, putting forth the power of the spirit to bring universal work of Christ for the salvation of the world nearer to its completion.[5]

The church's mission is to share with the world the good news that "God so loved the world" (John 3:16).

When my son was a small boy I learned anew a truth that I had discovered, though did not recognize, as a youngster myself. While working in the yard, I was suddenly aware of my small son's presence. On an impulse I turned and asked the youngster to help me with the task. My son seemed to grow six inches as he responded joyfully to being asked to help his father. I remembered the feeling when my own father had given me such a privilege.

The church must discover and each believer must sense the joy of the Father calling each of us into His task. The result of the gospel in our lives is to call us to be instruments in what God is about in this world.

Throughout church history there have been churches who were nearly oblivious to their mission. During the Reformation the early Reformers did not emphasize the mission of the church. At other times the church has been galvanized by that awareness. These are always periods of growth and health and excitement. When local congregations become aware of their mission, that mission often explains what is happening in their lives. Individual members find themselves as pilgrims and apostles in ways they never thought possible. All of this is not coincidental. The mission of the church is essential to understand who we are in Christ and what God is about in His grand plan of the ages.

Notes

1. J. Herbert Kane, *Understanding Christian Missions*, Bib 1972 3rd ed., pp. 107 *ff.*

2. "The Church in God's Plan" in Ralph Winter, ed., *Perspectives on the World Christian Movement, Howard A. Snyder p. 119.*

3. George F. Vicedom, *The Mission of God*, p. 56.

4. Arthur L. Walker, Jr., ed., *Educating for Christian Missions,* "The Rationale for Missions" Hugo H. Culpepper. p. 43.

5. Lesslie Newbigin, *The Open Secret: Sketches for a Missionary Theology* (Grand Rapids, Mich.: William B. Erdmans Publishing Company, 1978) p. 138.

2

The Commission of the Church

Mission, coming from the Latin word *mittere,* means to send. Mission is the total redemptive purpose of God, and God is both the Sender and the Sent in Christ. The church's mission is derived from God; all of its efforts to proclaim and to demonstrate the kingdom of God to the world is missions, the expression of its mission.

The church of the mission has a commission which gives the details of its mission. The commission arises not from a single passage of Scripture but from the whole thrust of biblical revelation. The crux of this revelation can be found in the passages called the Great Commission (Matt. 28:18-20; Mark 16:15-18; Luke 24: 46-49; John 20:21-23; 21:4-19; and Acts 2—8). The basic imperative we know as the Great Commission is most popularly cited from Matthew 28:18-20. A thorough study of that passage helps our understanding of the church's commission, but that passage should be seen only as the high point of a range of biblical thought, the crescendo of a symphony with movements played from the time of creation itself.

In the Old Testament

At the close of the creation section of the Book of Genesis, which many agree is the tenth chapter, there is an elementary listing of people, or nations. Of these Johannes Verkuyl has said:

> All of the nations issue forth from the creative hand of God and stand under His watchful eye of patience and judgment. The nations are not mere decorations incidental to the real drama between God and man; rather, the nations. . . that is, mankind as a whole—are part of the drama itself. God's work and activity are directed at the whole of humanity.[1]

The biblical revelation is sharply focused on the nations. God called Abraham and made a covenant with him. Through Abraham God would bless all the families of the earth. Abraham was to bring forth a people. The people were to become God's instruments in realization of His goals to reach all nations. Abraham's progeny would be His peculiar people for the task.

With the deliverance of that people from Egyptian captivity under the hands of Moses, God was ready for the next step. That peculiar people became Israel, "a chosen nation." God was in covenant with this nation. They were His people for His purpose.

Much of the Old Testament deals with this people's failure to keep that covenant and God's patient, long-suffering efforts to bring them back to it. That process laid the foundation for God's ultimate step in reaching the nations.

Winston Crawley said, "The tension between the missionary purpose of God and the lack of missionary vision and compassion on the part of God's people is well illustrated by the prophet Jonah."[2]

While Crawley only alluded to it, most readers will remember how Jonah resisted God's efforts to send him to the capital of the brutal, and barbaric Assyrian empire. Jonah fled toward Tarshish. A storm overtook him that put him in the belly of the great fish. Dramatic themes of God's concern for "all nations" emerge along with prophetic images of the death, burial, and resurrection of Jesus Christ.

Nineveh's repentance holds promise for the church's missionary efforts in the face of the most awesome resistance. In turn, Israel's disobedience not only indicted them but foreshadowed the church's too often acted out tendency to flee the responsibilities of its mission.

Jonah also teaches that God's purposes will not be thwarted. The groundwork was laid; when the fullness of time came, God sent forth His Son into the world. This was not a collapse of God's earlier plans but rather the fulfillment of all that He had done. Jesus Christ was the climax of God's covenant activity.

The Christ event establishes God's ultimate compassion and purpose for all nations. In the early stages of His ministry, Christ spoke of reaching into the heart of human misery "to preach good news to the poor. . . to proclaim freedom for the prisoners and recovery of sight for the blind, to release the oppressed, to proclaim the year of the Lord's favor" (Luke 4:18-19 , NIV). He was sent from the Father, and He began to call out those around Him who would become the foundation for a spiritual Israel, for a new "peculiar people" who would be His instrument for reaching "all the nations."

The Great Commission

Thus, it is not suprising that the church stopped at Matthew 28:18-20 as if it were an Ebenezer stone of old. It not only looks back to all that had gone before but also looks ahead in a new way to a new people.

> Jesus came up and spoke to them, saying, "All authority has been given to Me in heaven and on earth. Go therefore and make disciples of all nations, baptizing them in the name of the Father and the Son and the Holy Spirit, teaching them

to observe all that I commanded you; and lo, I am with you
always, even to the end of the age. (NASB).

Beyond Israel

The dramatic declaration that "all authority has been
given to Me in heaven and on earth" recognized the fact that
Jesus Christ is sovereign over all nations. The covenants with
Abraham and David with their promise of a universal and
everlasting kingdom and a sovereignty of righteousness were
fulfilled in Jesus Christ. An enthroned Lord, crucified and
risen, now issues His mandate to mission. His authority to
do so is undisputed, and His God-given purpose for all nations can be clearly delineated.

The idea is to bring all nations under Christ's discipline
and under the rule of the kingdom of God. While Jesus had
given almost all of His ministry to the "lost sheep of the
house of Israel" (Matt. 10:6), He clearly revealed that His
ministry now includes "all nations" (Matt 28:19). Theologians argue whether "all nations" means just the Gentiles or
also includes Israel. Undoubtedly, the focus is beyond Israel,
but that does not mean Israel is excluded. They are simply
swallowed up in the larger environment. The sons of Abraham must become spiritual sons in the same way any other
individual does.

Discipling the Nations

The word "nations" is the same word used in Revelation
5:9 to describe the inhabitants of New Jerusalem, the bride
of Christ, who come from "every tribe and tongue and people
and nation." Thus, "all nations" gives the passage clear intent of world conquest. It envisions an absolute commitment
to that task.

The command could only be received in the context of

Christ's assertion of the sovereignty God has committed to Him. "All authority in heaven and earth has been given to me."

"Go therefore" is led by a participle with the force of an imperative which sets up as the main focus of the Commission the "discipling of all nations." Obviously to disciple all nations the followers of Jesus Christ will have to go. It can be read "as you go" or as the King James Version and other translations have traditionally said, "Go ye therefore." The Greek word used means "to depart, to leave, to cross boundaries." Verkuyl said that means "sociological boundaries, racial boundaries, cultural boundaries and geographical boundaries." He added, "The missionary must always be willing and ready to cross boundaries whether they be at home or away."[3]

But the command to "make disciples of all nations" will continually pull the apostle of any generation across whatever boundaries stand in the way.

The commission is consistent with the announcement of the kingdom of God with which Jesus began His ministry. In essence, making disciples means bringing all nations under the rule of that kingdom. Literally, it means that all peoples would embrace Christ's discipline.

The great missions teacher, W. O. Carver, said of the kingdom theme:

> First of all, and always, the point of reference must be the ultimate objective. Jesus stated it for us in a number of terms, all reflecting one comprehensive purpose and passion.
>
> His constitutive concept from first to last was the kingdom of God or kingdom of heaven. To proclaim the reign and win obedience to the rule of God was to discharge the first duty to God and to serve the complete good of man.[4]

Bringing all nations under the authority and reign of Jesus

Christ can be understood as bringing the kingdom of God to expression among all people through proclamation and discipling. It is certainly the unifying theme for the mission of the church.

Baptizing and Teaching

On the strength of the authority declared, envisioning the boundary crossing inherent in it, the command is to disciple all nations, to bring them all under the rule of the King, to realize the kingdom of God in this world. This involves two simple strategies in the Great Commission: baptizing and teaching. Interestingly enough, neither aspect of this part of the Commission receives a great deal of emphasis from biblical commentators. Either they are assumed or they lose some of their emphasis under the dramatic impact of "discipling all nations."

Baptizing, of course, raises some traditional questions. Few New Testament scholars would argue that the word means to immerse and dramatizes the death, burial, and resurrection of Jesus Christ. Whether it has a role in completing salvation or primary significance as an act of obedience in response to salvation faith is not to be debated here. The point is that Jesus saw it as the first act in the discipling process.

The passage also contains the first Trinitarian formula, the introduction of the threefold nature of God as Father, Son, and Holy Spirit. The baptismal formula does not say "names" (plural), but "name" (singular). Father, Son, and Holy Spirit are thus seen as one, and this significance helped the early church integrate its understanding of the Godhead.

The relationship of baptism to Israel has been ignored by some. When Judaism reached out beyond the people of circumcision to the Gentiles in a proselytizing task, it prescribed the cleansing ritual of immersion. The baptizing process thus dramatizes the fact that all people are outside the circle of the "peculiar people of God" until they are brought in by Christ's redemptive act as reflected by their faith and baptism.

Baptism's accompanying call to teach includes more than the instruction that is so much a part of all missionary activity everywhere. Educational institutions that have grown up around the missionary task are often justified by this phrase. But the principle involved is much broader. The emphasis is to teach obedience. To observe all that Jesus commanded is consistent with the discipling idea of bringing all people and nations under the discipline of Jesus Christ. The teaching process envisions introducing a full awareness of just what such obedience involves. What is the yoke that the believer is asked to take upon oneself? What is involved?

The call to righteousness that John the Baptist sounded in the wilderness and which he punctuated with baptism upon evidence of repentance is brought forward at this point. The teachings of Jesus call people to a new kind of righteousness. Jesus' righteousness issues from the heart and is grounded in a person's spirit as it is made alive by the Holy Spirit.

All that Jesus taught about being in the kingdom of God is curriculum for the teaching side of the twofold strategy of discipling.

David Barrett said the Matthew 28:18-20 passage needs the balance of the Mark 16:15 account where the emphasis is more on preaching or evangelizing. Barrett pointed out that the Greek word *euangelizō* is used fifty-seven times in the New Testament. He said it means more than just speaking or preaching; it is proclamation with full authority and power. Barrett felt these two words contained in the Matthew and Mark accounts of the Great Commission require the comprehensive methodology that is inherent in the modern expression of the mission of the church.[5]

The Great Promise

The Great Commission ends here in the eyes of many and the "great promise" follows. But it is perhaps more correct to realize that the great promise is absolutely essential to the Great Commission. Christ can call His followers to such an awesome task with historical and eternal consequences because of His commitment to be with them. Does this presage Pentecost? Is this the promise that they were to wait on?

Many Christians feel that the revelation of an indwelling Christ through the coming of the Spirit is included here. That is probably true, yet it also means more. William O'Brien began his missionary career under appointment to Indonesia. Later he testified that on the long voyage across the Pacific he saw himself taking Christ to the Indonesians. But in Indonesia he found Christ already there, not just in terms of the missionaries who had preceded him, but in the cosmic activity of the Lord who called him and promised to be with him "always."

The Christian missionary crossing a new boundary finds that Christ has preceded him. Christ's indwelling presence manifests itself at the point at which a missionary decides to go. But the missionary quickly discovers that the Christ who said, "I am with you always" presides over the whole drama, not just his personal part.

Until the End

The phrase, "to the end of the age" (NASB) envisions Christ's return and the last days. But it also says Christians are not released from this task until then. No whistle will blow to give relief from the crusade short of His return. The task is not finished, no matter how complete it might seem at any point in time, until the Master has come to claim His people and to establish His authority over "all nations."

The Great Commission is Christ centered rather than man centered. Despite the overwhelming command encompassing all nations and all time, the emphasis is upon Christ who has received all authority, who will be present throughout the task, who will provide the power for it, and whose return will complete it.

The mandate for missions that is known as the Great Commission cannot be understated even though it must not be left standing alone. Throughout Christian history, it has been the marching orders of the church.

> It has literally molded religious and social patterns for two thousand years. It cradles the inherent concepts of divine authority, world evangelization, church fellowship, church education, ethical and moral responsibility, assurance of divine presence and anticipation of the consummation of the age.[6]

Elsewhere in the New Testament

The Great Commission does not stand alone in the New Testament in developing the theology of mission or laying the groundwork for the mission of the church. There are key verses that state or expand upon the same great truth.

While the Great Commission and the various Scriptures that relate to it constitute the crux of the church's mission and its understanding of its mission, the life of Jesus constantly spelled out in dynamic form the nature of the mission that His followers inherit.

In Matthew 6:9 and following, He taught them to pray a prayer that focused on their mission, "Thy will be done, On earth as it is in heaven." In Matthew 10:5-15 Christ sent the twelve disciples out to announce that the "kingdom of heaven is at hand" (v.7), and in Luke 10:1-20 the seventy went out with the message of the kingdom. The church is being gathered, and there is no doubt in the life and teachings of Jesus Christ that the church has a mission.

In Matthew 16:18-19 the exchange at Caesarea Philippi focuses directly on the church ". . .and on this rock I will build my church and the powers of [hell] shall not prevail against it. I will give you the keys of the kingdom of heaven."

Jesus' postcrucifixion and resurrection appearances, of course, led to the passages that constitute the Great Commission. But John 20:21 is the statement that " as my Father hath sent me, even so send I you" (KJV). Few passages so clearly point out the trail of the mission from Father, to Son, to disciple. The dimension of sending anticipates every border crossing that might be encountered to "all nations."

Christ tied the Commission to the coming of the Holy Spirit. In Acts 1:8, the risen Lord focused on a mission that was such that they would need to "[wait] for power from on high" (Luke 24:49). After Pentecost (Acts 2:1-47) the preaching that resulted from the infilling of the Holy Spirit was replete with a mission consciousness, (Acts 2:37-47).

Paul's life, as introduced in Acts 9, was galvanized by that sense of mission. Ananias was told by the Lord to go to Paul, "for he is a chosen instrument of mine to carry my name before the Gentiles and kings and the sons of Israel" (v. 15).

In 1 Corinthians 2, Paul spoke of his mission in terms of the proclamation of Jesus Christ as the crucified Lord. And the course of his ministry, as spelled out throughout the Book of Acts, was that of a man who knew that he and the church had received a mission from the risen and sovereign Lord.

When Paul wrote Ephesians, his sense of the mission of the church was largely complete and he was able to say,

> For he has made known to us in all wisdom and insight the mystery of his will, according to his purpose which he set

forth in Christ as a plan for the fulness of time, to unite all things in him, things in heaven and things on earth" (Eph. 1:9-10).

In verse 12, Paul added, "We who first hoped in Christ have been destined and appointed to live for the praise of his glory."

Many theologians feel that Paul's insights in Ephesians 3:1-13 were the highest point of his understanding of the church's purpose and its mission. Here Paul spelled out God's eternal purpose. He laid open the secret. The nations or Gentiles were joint heirs and the church was the instrument through which God had purposed to make this grand event known.

Hugo Culpepper said, "The apostle Paul permitted the mission of the church to come to a focus in his life."[7] This truth is seen in Colossians 1:24-29,

> Now I rejoice in my sufferings for your sake, and in my flesh I complete what is lacking in Christ's afflictions for the sake of his body, that is, the church, of which I became a minister according to the divine office which was given to me for you, to make the word of God fully known, the mystery hidden for ages and generations but now made manifest to his saints. To them God chose to make known how great among the Gentile are the riches of the glory of this mystery, which is Christ in you, the hope of glory. Him we proclaim, warning every man and teaching every man in all wisdom, that we may present every man mature in Christ. For this I toil, striving with all the energy which he mightily inspires within me.

The Pervasive Theme

The mission of the church is to make Jesus Christ known to the world. In fact, He came to do what He did so that we might do what now lies before us. God's mission, entrusted to His Son, and through the Son to the church, is the church's mission until the end of the age.

The mission began with creation itself. God's purposes have been persistent for all time. The amazing truth of the church is that it has been called into being by God's mission and commissioned through Jesus Christ to realize this great purpose.

The mission of the church is a pervasive theme that runs from Genesis through Revelation. It moves majestically from Abraham to Israel to Christ where it culminates and brings forth a new covenant people. The new covenant is not restricted to a nation but is composed of all believers everywhere. The secret is laid open and the effort is joined and the task clearly is set before the church.

Is the church aware of its commission and its mission in the latter years of this twentieth century? After two centuries of unprecedented missionary activity, one would think so. But as David Barrett pointed out in his booklet, *World-Class Cities and World Evangelization,* the progress that followed the modern missionary era is now being eclipsed by population explosions, resurgent old religions, and the seductive secularizing of a large part of the Christian church.[8]

One way for a believer to approach the question of how compelling Christ's mission is to the modern church is to look at his or her own congregation. Is the fellowship of believers with whom you gather, with whom you worship, with whom you affirm Christ's purposes in time and eternity, deeply conscious of its commission? Is it something given only lip service or does it galvanize the resources and the spiritual gifts that are obvious in individual members? Does it come to grips with the unique opportunities surrounding the church's location in the midst of one of the nations to be discipled?

A review of the march of the church's mission from the early days of the Commission till now might help set a context for answering that question in more concrete terms.

Notes

1. Johannes Verkuyl, "The Biblical Foundation for the Worldwide Mission Mandate" in Ralph D. Winter, ed. *Perspectives On the World Christian Movement,* pp. 35-36.

2. Winston Crawley, *Global Mission: A Story to Tell,* p. 78.

3. Verkuyl, p. 49.

4. William O. Carver, *Christian Mission in Today's World* (Nashville: Boardman Press, 1942), p. 61.

5. David B. Barrett, *World-Class Cities and World Evangelization,* p. 9.

6. Bill Austin, *Austin's Topical History of Christianity,* p. 42.

7. Hugo H. Culpepper, "The Rationale for Missions," in Arthur L. Walker, Jr., ed. *Education for Christian Missions,* p. 41.

8. Barrett, p. 10.

3

The March of Mission

Understanding the church's mission requires some analysis of the ebb and flow of its fortunes from the days of its biblical commissioning to the present. While church history provides the data for such an analysis it rarely is an analysis in itself.

> For the most part, church history is concerned with Christian doctrine, ecclesiastical machinery, church feuds, schismatic movements, ecumenial councils, papal bulls, imperial decrees, religious wars, the exercise of discipline, the formulation of creeds, the suppression of heresy, and other episodes and movements relating to the survival and success of the church as a gigantic religions institution. Little or nothing is said about the preaching of the gospel, the translation and distribution of the Scriptures, the conversion of non-Christian peoples, or the extension of the kingdom into all parts of the world.[1]

The church often seems to have been battered back and forth by larger currents of history. Of course, the concept of a sovereign God who rules over the affairs of human beings suggests that the fortunes of the church's mission are more central to history than a secularist would ever suspect.

The burden of this chapter is to review how the mission of the church has been expressed and perceived throughout history. This chapter will deal selectively with events related to the church's mission. A look at the political point of view follows because political structures have been important in the way the church has expressed its mission.

The church's history will also be examined to see how church structures have affected its view of mission and the way it has carried out that mission. Finally the impact of geography on the church's mission will be briefly discussed.

Historical Review

The church that gathered in Jerusalem awaiting Pentecost did not have a clear vision of mission. But immediately after Pentecost, church and mission began to look like fire and its burning. Two ways to follow the mission of the church in the first century are to review its geographical centers and to follow the traditions of its major personalities.

Geographical Centers

The three chief centers for Christian mission during the apostolic age were Jerusalem, Antioch, and Ephesus. This will surprise some people who want to focus on Rome as a center, at least from Nero's persecutions onward. More likely Rome's lowest point began at the end of the first century AD.

Jerusalem was obviously the first center. Witnesses to the kingdom of God, made possible through Jesus Christ's death and resurrection, went out in every direction not only in the course of commerce but also under pressure of persecution. More than likely missionary zeal took a backseat to these two more practical elements.

The fact that Jerusalem was the center of early mission activity is underscored by the first apostolic council. There the question of what Jewish influence would carry over into Christian discipling was confronted. This dealt with the problem of the Judaizers who had dogged Paul's steps. The decision by the council was that the gospel was not warmed-over Judaism.[2] Jerusalem was considered the home of the mother church at this point.

The impetus for mission, however, quickly switched from Jerusalem to Antioch. In part this was because of the much-heralded mission enterprises of Paul and Barnabas and, in part, because it was a natural jumping-off place for movement into Asia Minor and on toward Greece and Rome.

The third center for mission effort in the first century of Christendom was Ephesus.[3] Paul gave a great deal of his time to establishing the church in Ephesus, and there he began to defend the church's doctrinal purity against the waves of change that would come through the centuries. Another reason Ephesus assumed such importance was that the apostle John made Ephesus his base in the latter days of his life.

Antioch and Ephesus became more important when Jerusalem was all but eliminated as a Christian center by the Jewish wars that culmated in Jerusalem's destruction in AD 70. Many Christians, trying to establish their separation from Judaism, moved out just prior to its destruction.[4]

Dominant Personalities

Paul, often called the thirteenth apostle, met Jesus in a Damascus Road experience. He was the dominant mission personality in the first century of Christian history. Paul, who had initially persecuted Christians, found only reluctant acceptance from the disciples at first.[5] But, along with Barnabas, he proved himself in mission endeavors in Asia Minor and Greece and was vindicated at the Jerusalem conference.

Sometime after Paul's pioneering work in Ephesus, John established his base there. Except for the time he was banished to Patmos during one of the many persecutions that began to dog Christian efforts, John made Ephesus a center of influence for the new Christian religion. He probably wrote his Gospel and Epistles in Ephesus.

James, of course, was the brother of John and the first Christian martyr, (Acts 12:2). James the brother of Jesus and the pastor of the Jerusalem flock was conservative and reluctant to abandon Jewish traditions. Yet his compromise carved the way for the mission enterprise at the Jerusalem conference (Acts 15:13-21).

Tradition focuses on Peter in and around Jerusalem and later in Rome. Andrew is traditionally believed to have died in Scythia, giving Christianity its first move toward the north. Bartholomew is tied in with India, as is Thomas. Matthew is understood to have been throughly committed to missions. Tradition has him martyred in either Ethiopia or Persia.

The ministries of James Alphaeus and Simon Zelotes included Egypt. Simon Zelotes is also tied with early ministries in Britain. Philip witnessed in Greece, and John Mark moved on to North Africa.

No matter how we look at the first century, whether from centers of activity or dominant personalities, the excitement of the Christian message was like spilt milk. It went in every direction. While some churches, uniquely that at Antioch, had a strong sense of mission, the most common mission experience came as believers simply shared their faith as life's currents carried them about. In that sense a Great Commission reading "as you go" rather than the imperative "go" might more nearly describe the mission of the church in the first century.

Advance Through Adversity

Christianity, winsome with its freshness and enlivened by its opposition, moved into the second century of its existence as a tiny minority. Yet it must have grown quickly, for from AD 100 to 312 it experienced wave after wave of persecution. The persecutions began under Nero in the mid-sixties and concluded with Diocletian in 303. Instead of suppressing or eliminating Christianity, persecution became a catalyst for something dramatically different.

During this period the mission of the church was not nearly as dominant as was the church taking form. The church began to articulate its doctrines and beliefs, dealt with its first heresies and schisms, and developed a group of leaders so influential that historians have since called them "the Church Fathers." But the period is also set apart by a series of persecutions. Each persecution had a major martyr and often a major leader. More often than not the major leaders turned out to be the martyrs. Much Christian writing was done which circulated with a strong missionary momentum. At times the writings sparked major controversies over what was orthodox and what was heresy. The writers who were more accepted by Christians were called the patricians or apostolic fathers.

Another group developed during this period. "Apologists" directed themselves specifically to unbelievers. They included such names as Aristides around 120, Justin Martyr around 130, Tatian around 160, Athenagoras around 177, and Theophilus in the same period. Such names as Irenaeus, Tertullian, Clement of Alexandria, and Origen dominated the next two centuries. Origen addressed the church more directly than the world.

By this time Rome had become one of the major centers of the Christian mission, along with Alexandria and Carthage in North Africa. The persecutions that flourished during this period probably reflected the progress of Christian growth throughout the Roman Empire. They also represented constant miscalculation on the part of Roman authorities on how pervasive Christianity had become.

A State Church

Christianity, which had been an illegal religion through its first three centuries became legal, respectable, and dominant in one major battle. The change was wrought by a man named Constantine. He became emperor of Rome in 312 after leading his troops to victory over a rival under the Christian sign, following a unique dream.

Christianity had become so pervasive following the Diocletian persecution that Emperor Galerius issued an eddict of toleration toward Christianity in 311 and declared it legal. When Constantine declared himself a convert from the religion of helios, the sun god, to Christianity, he set off a debate unresolved to this day. What were the true motives of his conversion? Did he simply recognize that the cross of Christ had already carried the day and therefore adopted it, or was he truly impressed, as many say, with the order and morality of Christian life? Like other Christians of that day, he delayed his own baptism until his approaching death, believing that would take care of the majority of sins in his life.

The mission of the church changed radically with its new status under Constantine. Before, its mission had been performed in the face of persecution. Now, it seemed to have a free hand. Everybody wanted to climb aboard, and the question of genuine conversion became critical. Paganism was a tenacious enemy and seemed to assert itself even under the cloak of Christianity.

The spread of Christianity was effected by an early division in this new state-sanctioned church. Constantine set the atmosphere when he allowed the bishop of Rome to resolve a doctrinal matter in the Donatists' controversy. Following the Diocletian persecutions, many Christian leaders who had been forced to turn over Christian Scriptures to the authorities found their positions and validity as spiritual leaders questioned by others led by a bishop named Donatus. When the bishop of Rome ruled against them with Constantine's support, the role of the bishop of Rome was greatly strengthened. He would increasingly assert his primacy among his peers, though not in the sense of the Papacy which developed later.

In 325 Constantine convened Christian bishops in Nicea to try to work through still another division within the Christian community. The question centered on the person of Jesus Christ—whether He was divine and not human or both divine and human. Apart from the theological decisions which so galvanized the church, the gathering of leaders gave the church a new awareness of itself and a new sense of mission. The victims had become victors, as one historian put it, but they rode off in every direction from that victory.

Ironically controversies also became an impetus for mission. The spreading of the good news, however, was somewhat secondary to the spreading of the particular point of view by an individual leader or from an individual center.

In 330 Constantine moved his capital to the site of an ancient fortress town called Byzantium, now the modern city of Istanbul. It was known for the centuries between as Constantinople or the city of Constantine.

After Constantine's death, the Roman Empire began to fall into deep division as Rome was sacked by invaders again and again. Both Constantinople in the East and Rome in the West became centers for mission, but each took a different form. The destruction of civil powers in Rome by the invading barbarians actually increased the strength of religious powers. In Constantinople the civil and religious leaders remained more allied.

In the years that followed the development of these two

centers, many Christian leaders emerged who helped the church define its mission. One of the most influential was Augustine, who lived from 354 to 430 and who came from North Africa. Among other things, Augustine helped articulate the church's concept of its relationship to the state in a way that would allow it to move freely as a state church and feel justified in using the state's power to accomplish its ends.

By the mid-400s the Roman bishop Leo the First claimed for himself papal rights which the Catholic Church cherishes to this very day. He gave the mission of the church a new framework by expanding his influence into Africa, Spain, and what is now France. His successors were extremely missionary, but their driving motivation was the primacy of their authority.

During this period as a state church, however, Christianity developed new mission centers from a reactionary source. Monasticism developed as a reaction to the churches becoming wealthy, privileged, and, too often, corrupt. Monasticism was the gathering of pious men who renounced wealth and privilege, and even marriage, to devote themselves to the study of the Scriptures and to prayer. Such devotion propelled them into missions to preach the gospel or to serve humanity in the most humble ways. They became the first clearly delineated missionaries since Paul's day. They took vows of poverty, chastity, and obedience, and their daily activities were prayer and work. They constituted the most formidable mission movement since the days of the early church.

These monks, as they were called, established missionary centers in what is now England, Scotland, and Ireland and began to influence pagan Europe from these centers, a kind of second front of missions.

Challenge from the East

In the years that followed, missions made strong inroads in Western Europe but faced a threating tide from the East.

Historian Will Durant identified that tide as a great new religious force called Islam which arose in the seventh century, following the death of its founder, Muhammad, in 632. Durant said, "The explosion of the Arabrian peninsular into the conquest and conversion of half the Mediterranean is the most extraordinary phenomenon in medieval history."[6]

The ancient Bible lands were conquered within a few years. By 650 Persia was under Islamic control and by the first part of the 700s North Africa and Spain echoed with the sound of Muslim calls to prayer.

Islam began its assault on Europe from Spain. But as the Muslims crossed the Pyrenees in 732, they were stopped by a coalition of Europeans under the leadership of Charles Martel at the Battle of Tours.

Martel's victory gave rise to a new dimension among Christian forces in the West through his grandson Charles the Great, or as he is better known, Charlemagne. This charismatic and pious prince set up a new alliance with the Roman bishop, now calling himself pope, and called it the Holy Roman Empire.

Charlemagne and his successors strengthened the influence of Roman Christianity as Eastern Christianity was cut off by Muhammadan advances. Mission efforts in Europe continued in Scandinavia with such leaders as Anskar in the mid-800s. Denmark, Sweden, and Norway were reached again a century and a half later through the influence of British missions.

The mission efforts that reverberated from Britain back to the Northern European continent were a spiritual contrast to the bloody march of the Muhammadans during the seventh

century. The British Christian churches, themselves the result of the missionary campaigns of such leaders as Gregory
and Augustine around 600, heard the call to European missions from Wilfrid in the late 600s.[7] One of his prodigies,
Willibrord of Northumbria, began preaching in what is now
the Netherlands in AD 690. He set up a cathedral outside
Utrecht and built a monastery in Luxembourg which itself
became a missionary center.

One of Willibrord's collaborators, known as Boniface,
secured from the pope in Rome a personal commission to
evangelize the people of Germany. He was ordained a missionary bishop to Germany in 722 and furthered Christian
witness in what is now Switzerland, southern Germany, and
western Austria. Called by many the greatest missionary
since the apostle Paul, Boniface was waylaid and killed by
robbers in 1754.

Eastern Christianity also fostered mission efforts during
this period from its center in Constantinople. In the mid-800s
missionaries were sent to what is now Moravia. Successors
to that mission were effective in Bohemia and Hungary and
as far north as Poland. Though most of the missionary effort
in this area was initiated by Eastern missionaries, a large
portion of Slavic Christianity soon turned to Rome for its
leadership.

On the Offensive

From 1066, when William the Conqueror led the Nor-
mans across the channel to subdue Britain, to 1453, when
Constantinople was captured by the Ottoman Turks, Christian mission seemed to be in constant reaction to the great
Muslim challenge. European-based Crusades were mounted
in 1096, 1147, 1188, and 1202. These efforts on the part of
well-meaning Christians to retake holy places from the Mus-

lim invaders represented a mission spirit all but canceled by a brutal militancy and the lure of Eastern wealth.

In retrospect, these were sad days for the cause of Christian missions. The capture of Jerusalem in 1099, in which not even women and children were spared, gave Christianity a bloody and hated role in Muslim history. From that point missions to Muslims have been difficult.

While others attempted different approaches to Muslim missions, none met with success. Yet, the great Catholic thinker, Thomas Aquinas, who spent so much time wedding theology and Aristotelian logic, produced one of his great works in an attempt to equip missionaries to make an effective witness with Muslims.

One of the major Christian controversies that divided the East and West, called the Iconoclastic Controversy, focused on the icons or images or statues so popular in Western Christianity. It arose because Eastern Christians saw them as an offense to Muslims and something that stood in the way of reaching Muslims. The Eastern church tried but failed to impose their convictions on the Western churches. Roman ascendency was assured when Constantinople fell to the Muslims in the mid-1400s.

Efforts to Reform and Renew

Even though Rome had triumphed over the East, it found itself caught in another schism; this one involved the pope in Rome and a rival one in France. It was a period of religious and spiritual corruption. Cries for reform began to be heard, especially in Europe. These would have dramatic impact on the missionary vision of the church in the years that followed.

Early reformers such as John Wycliffe translated the Bible and gave it to unlicensed preachers called Lollards. The derisive term meant "mumblers." Though they had a strong mission emphasis, their efforts were more in the area of reform. The reaction from the Papacy included heavy persecution and even burning at the stake.

Another early reformer was John Huss. Active in the early 1400s in Bohemia, Huss questioned the absolute authority of the pope and championed the rights of the laity.

All of this stimulated mission activity somewhat but seemed to prepare European Christendom for the reform that revolved around Martin Luther in the early 1500s. Luther's nailing his ninety-five theses, challenging Rome, to the church door at Wittenburg Castle on October 31, 1517, is generally acknowledged as the beginning of the Protestant Reformation.

While the Reformation stimulated both Protestant and Catholic missions in subsequent centuries, the Protestant Reformers were not, in themselves, mission minded. As J. Herbert Kane pointed out, the Reformers taught that the Great Commission pertained only to the original apostles and that the church really had no responsibility to send missionaries further than had already been sent during the apostolic age.[8] Too, the Protestant churches were so weakened by their efforts to confront force and counterreform efforts by Roman Catholics and the wars that came on the heels of the Reformation that their problem was more one of survival than missions. When Roman Catholic missions began to ride the tide of Spanish and Portuguese explorations into the New World, Protestantism was locked into Protestant Europe.[9]

Roman Catholic missions surged dramatically during the postreform movement. In part, it was due to the strong maritime efforts of predominately Catholic countries, such as Spain, Portugual, and Italy. However, it was also due to the development of religious orders in the Roman Catholic

Church, such as the Franciscans, and later the Jesuits, that provided vibrant centers for missionary outreach.

The direction reforms took in Scandinavia and in Britain differed from other European countries. From them came two of the most influencial centers in modern missions. Strong pietistic movements in Denmark led to a missionary effort in the East Indies; the Moravians, whose beginnings go back to John Huss, began a mission in the Virgin Islands and later in Greenland before including Latin America, South Africa, and North America.

In England the Church of England had broken away from Rome and, in turn, had seen congregational groups break away from it. A strong sense of mission developed early in both the Church of England and the various congregational bodies that spun off from it.

Modern Missions

The year 1792 marks the beginning of modern missions under the inspiration of a Baptist cobbler named William Carey. Carey, inspired by the voyages of Captain Cook, abandoned shoe-making to begin missionary work in India. Carey's example soon attracted followers from North America. Congregational missionaries Adoniram and Ann Judson and Luther Rice became Baptists and worked in India and then began work in Burma.

Kenneth Scott Latourette called the nineteenth century "the great century" in the expansion of Christianity. Eastern Orthodox, Roman Catholic, and Protestant missions surged forward around the world.

Political Analysis

Christian missions cannot be divorced from the political environment in which it has operated from the earliest days. Christian historians even talk about the role of political movements in preparations for the coming of Christ (that is, the fullness of time). Alexander's Greece had provided a language and had unified diverse nations around the great Mediterranean basin stretching from India to Spain. Roman conquest had absorbed Greek thinking and expanded the empire, providing the *Pax Romana* or peace of Rome and the roads that allowed free movement. Thus, when Christianity appeared it found an atmosphere in which it could easily transcend national borders and indigenous languages.

Roman Role

Roman rule provided the environment for the spread of Christianity and inadvertently fanned its flames by trying to stamp it out. The Roman persecutions that dominated the first three centuries further scattered the Christian witness. Mission was often underground during this period but was more vibrant as a result. Martyrdom exerted a powerfully cleansing effect on the quality of discipleship.

A second aspect of Roman rule was that when Christianity suddenly became the religion of the land following Constantine's ascendency, it had a ready tide on which to ride. While the quality of discipleship declined, Christian churches multiplied. Christian thinkers arose, and Christian missions, ever inherent in the Christian experience, rode the fortunes of the Roman world.

The Breakup of Rome

The church grew even stronger as the state that had given it such a boost began to decline. Successive waves of pagan attacks caused Christians to realize how important it was to evangelize these people. Efforts on the part of Christian political leaders to mount missions to the homelands of their would-be conquerors achieved early successes that laid the groundwork for the Christianization of Europe.

East and West Division

The division of the Roman Empire into eastern and western centers at Rome and Constantinople divided the early church also. Rome and Constantinople became two major centers for mission. The eastern center became the base for much of the evangelization of what is now known as the European Communist world; Rome became the center for mission for what is now the Western European world.

Holy Roman Empire

After Charles Martel stopped the Muhammadans at Tours in 732, Charlemagne received the church's sanction as a new Roman emperor. This provided the Roman church a golden opportunity to establish its primacy over the state. It enjoyed this role to varying degrees over the centuries in Europe and in other countries where it was predominant. At the same time, the Roman church depended on political structures to enforce its power and expand its borders.

The Rise of European States

The Holy Roman Empire broke up, however, as French, German, Spanish, and English nationalism became strong enough to enable the people to assert their independence from Roman control. This laid the groundwork for the Reformation, which could only truly flourish when the Roman church did not control all the heads of state. The European states gained political stability and began building empires.

Colonial Tides

The mission of the church rode the tides of colonial expansionism into the modern era of missions. Roman Catholic missions rode on the heels of the explorers and flags of Spain and Portugal. For Protestants, missions followed the fortunes of the Netherlands and Britain. Indeed, the expansion of Christianity during this period followed the flags of these various political entities.

The Modern Era

Political realities have also dominated Christian missions in the modern era of nationalism. Communism, a nineteenth-century addition to political structures, provides the greatest challenge to Christianity since Islam. While Christianity has not been purged from Communist countries, its activities have been sharply limited with regard to missions.

Western democracies have become sources for modern mission efforts with their emphasis on guaranteed travel and protection of citizens under the passports of their orgin. The third world countries which have grown up between Western democracies and Communist countries have constituted a kind of prize for missionary efforts by both groups.

Ecclesiastical Dimensions

Another way to examine the march of missions in the period since the church first understood its calling is from an ecclesiastical point of view.

Pre-Catholic Centers

The earliest mission centers were based in Jerusalem, Antioch, Ephesus, and then Alexandria, Carthage, Rome, and Constantinople. Some of these centers gained prominence from the sheer numbers of Christians in their areas, and some of them developed from the force of individual leaders. But the churches in these centers were the early ecclesiastical structures that fueled the church's expansion and served as bases for its mission.

Western Christianity

The mighty Roman Catholic Church dominated Western European Christianity from about the fifth century. The Roman church sponsored missionary activities and where dissent arose was ferocious in squelching it.

From time to time reform would arise from the monasteries, yet other monastic orders were used by the church to squelch reform. In reaction to the Protestant Reformation, Roman Catholicism reasserted itself through monastic orders, especially through the followers of Ignatius Loyola who were called Jesuits. They took their faith to all parts of the world by identifying with the flag and traveling with Spanish and Portuguese explorers. Roman Catholic orders continue to be the center of their mission efforts in the modern era.

Eastern Christianity

When the church at Constantinople lost power to the church at Rome, the resulting Eastern church went its own way. More heavily influenced by Islam than Roman Catholicism, the Eastern church directed most of its mission efforts toward the north and away from the Muslim invaders. Except for its Mediterranean centers, the East was essentially landlocked and, therefore, never attempted the worldwide mission that Roman Catholicism undertook. The East's major mission efforts were into the Slavic countries and north to what is now the Soviet Union.

Lutherans

As noted in the historical review, Lutheran reformers were not initially missionary in nature. Only after pietistic elements began to develop in the Netherlands did a Lutheran missionary spirit emerge. Lutheran missions also followed flags planted by Germany in East Africa and by the Netherlands in the South sea islands of the Pacific. But since Lutheran countries did not reach the colonial strength of other countries, additional mission activity was limited to the migration of their peoples to such places as the midsection of the United States.

The Reform Churches

Reform churches emerged from John Calvin's slant on the Reformation, including the Church of Scotland and what was later called the Presbyterian Church. Their mission activity would seem to have been limited by their theology of election, but they developed many strong missionaries, not the least of whom was the great African explorer David Livingstone. In the modern era of missions, many missionaries in the nondenominational mission sector have emerged from reformed traditions and have served with great zeal, especially in Africa and the Orient.

The Church of England

The Church of England not only spawned mission-minded dissent from within itself, expressed in such church groups as Baptists, Methodists, and Congregationalists, but also had a strong mission emphasis in its own right. British colonialism paved the way for Church of England missions to the New World, to Africa, and to Asia. Some of the early Christian mission societies developed around the Church of England, though, like the Lutherans, it can be said to have followed its own people first and branched out from their colonies.

Baptists, Methodists, and Congregationalists

Probably the most zealous missionaries came from the ecclesiastical structures that spun off the English reform movement. Baptists, as we have already seen, led the way with William Carey's example in India and continued with the missionary efforts of Adonairam Judson in Burma and those who supported him. Methodists became great missionaries not only in the New World with the example of their founder, John Wesley, but also through their American churches became strong missionaries throughout the world. Congregationalists had their missionary heyday in the New World, and especially in New England, before losing their impetus to other mission entities.

Independents

In America in the 1800s, strong evangelistic activities spawned many nondenominational groups around such leaders as Dwight L. Moody. The Bible institute that he founded became a strong center for mission activity for independent churches and what were later called Bible churches. Many of the independent societies that we shall review later emerged from the strong missionary spirit that still flourishes in these groups.

Restorationists

Christian churches and later the Churches of Christ which developed in a movement called the Restoration Movement (an effort to get back to the purity of the New Testament and New Testament terminology) also have had a strong mission spirit in the modern period. The Christian church has not only spawned its own mission groups but has participated in many of the independent movements. The Churches of Christ have had a latter-day mission movement very tightly developed around their own unique structures.

Pentecostals

In the early 1900s the charismatic movement began with a renewed emphasis on the Holy Spirit and special evidences of His blessing in the lives of believers. Pentecostals, as they were often called, became strong missionaries in the post-World War II period and have been especially effective in the northern tier of countries in Latin America.

Summary

While ecclesiastical dimensions do not explain completely the church's mission activity through the years, much of what has been done has been under the sponsorship of one of these entities. They represent one form of the connection-alism which will be discussed in a later chapter as a method of mission.

Geographical Dimensions

The geographical point of view remains to complete a context for understanding the mission of the church as it has been perceived and carried out by believers through the centuries since Christ called His followers to the task. A review of the march of mission in each major area of the world will set the stage for a more definitive look at the mission of the church as it involves believers and churches today.

Asia

Tradition says India was reached by Christian missionaries, such as Thomas, in the first century. A Christian group called the Nestorians were supposed to have reached India and China during the first 200 years of the Christian experience. Roman Catholic missionaries were there in the period following the explorations of Marco Polo. Franciscans were in China in the fourteenth century. Jesuits were in India and Japan in the sixteenth century. They began their work in China in the 1600s.

At the close of the 1700s and early 1800s, Protestant missions began to assert themselves in China; during the 1920s, there were more than 15,000 missionaries in China. About half were Catholic and half Protestant.

Asia has probably been the scene of more heroic modern mission efforts than any other area. Many missionaries died as martyrs, and many more were felled by disease and privation. But missionaries kept going and established churches throughout the area. Yet Christians are a decided minority in Asia, considering such a vast investment in lives and resources. With the exception of the Philippines, where Roman Catholics made dramatic advances through their Spanish influence, and Korea where Protestant missions, especially those led by Presbyterians achieved their greatest results, Christians are tiny minorities in most Asian countries. Indonesia would be the nearest thing to an exception where nearly 10 percent of the people have become Christians and where Lutherans pioneered the way.

Overall, however, Asian Christians are less than 3 percent of the total population after 500 years of mission effort.

Africa

Missions to Africa began early with incursions into Egypt and what is now known as Ethiopia. The resulting Coptic Church is probably the oldest established example of Christian churches to be found anywhere, though it certainly does not resemble the larger streams of Christian life. During the early years, Christian missionaries and influence spread across North Africa, and two of the great centers of early Christian thought were Alexandria and Carthage. The initial wave of Muslim conquest, however, all but wiped out North African Christendom and was one reason the Coptic Church remained so isolated.

Roman Catholic missionaries accompanying Portuguese explorers refocused on Africa as a mission field in the 1400s. They established missions in West Africa and further south in the areas known as the Congo and Angola. The loss of colonies by Spain and Portugal, however, erroded their missionary efforts; by the eighteenth century, there were only small enclaves. The same society that sent William Carey to India sent missionaries to the west coast of Africa in the late 1700s and the early 1800s. British societies, a Reformed mission from Switzerland, and several American mission groups pioneered in the western part of Africa in the same period.

Further south, mission activity was highlighted by the work of Robert and Mary Smith Moffatt and David and Mary Moffat Livingstone. In East Africa, British and German missionaries worked to establish bases in the beautiful African highlands.

According to Herbert Kane, central Africa was opened up more by exploration and commerce through the Congo River than by Christian mission. In much of Africa, missions in the 1800s was a story of incredible privation and heavy losses to death by disease. In the early 1900s mission activities in Africa really began to pay off, however, and from 1900 to 1950 the Christian population there increased sixty times over. Despite new insurgencies by Islam from the north, the Christian response in Africa continues to be dramatic.

In recent years the number of Christians that have developed around Protestant missions numbers 75 million while Roman Catholic missions claim 80 million. Coptic Christians claim about 15 million adherents. Another 20 million are related to independent missions or uniquely African versions of Christianity.

Latin America

Latin America has been dominated by Catholic missions since the sixteenth century. Led by Franciscans and Dominicans in the early 1500s major Catholic enclaves were established in Brazil, Haiti, and Mexico followed by Cuba, Colombia, and Peru. During the second half of the 1500s most of the rest of Latin America was reached by Spanish explorers and dedicated Catholic missioners.

The cause of missions, however, suffered greatly under the greed of commerce and industry. Disease, enforced labor, and slavery wrought near genocide in certain areas.

As political reverses came for Spain and Portugal in the New World, Roman Catholicism had to scramble against major opposition from new governments before it reasserted its strength on a country-by-country basis. Through agreements with Rome, called concordats, Catholics managed to secure preferential treatment in most of the Latin American countries. In many of these countries the Roman Catholic population still exceeds 90 percent. The 90 percent, however, often includes less than 10 percent practicing. However, this is not a condition limited to Roman Catholics among Christians around the world.

Europe

Since much of early Christian mission focused in Europe, it is sad to point out that the strength of the churches in Europe has declined severely in the 1900s. Many mission groups are beginning to regard Europe as a new mission field. A number of major church missions from the United States have refocused their efforts on Europe in a kind of reverse mission story. On the other hand, strong church groups in England and Germany among Protestants and in France, Spain, and Italy among Roman Catholics continue to generate mission activity toward the traditional mission continents.

North America

Missions in North America began with the Spanish colonists from the South but received its major impetus from the

Puritan and Reform groups in the Northeast in what became known as New England. Baptists and Methodists led the way into the pioneer areas of the new world on the strength of two Great Awakenings or revivals. The religious movements generated tremendous mission endeavors by a variety of church groups led largely by untrained but fervent and often self-appointed missionaries.

Their success can be seen in the amount of mission activity now emerging from North America to all parts of the world.

Notes

1. J. Herbert Kane, *A Global View of Christian Missions,* rev. ed.., p. vii.

2. See Acts 15 for a recounting of the Jerusalem Conference.

3. "At the outset, Christianity was predominately urban. In moved along the trade routes from city to city. By the second decade of its second century in at least some parts of Asia Minor it had spread widely into towns and even into the countryside, but as strength was in the cities which were such prominent a feature of the Roman Empire." Kenneth Scott Latourette, *A History of Christianity,* 1:75.

4. Bill Austin, *Austin's Topical History of Christianity,* p. 54.

5. Acts 9 tells the story of Paul's early days and his conversion.

6. Will Durant, *The Age of Faith* (New York: Simon and Schuster, 1950), p. 155.

7. Gregory really articulated the papal concept for the Bishop of Rome first claimed by Leo I in AD 440.

8. J. Herbert Kane, *Understanding Christian Missions,* 3rd ed., p. 140.

9. Ibid.

4

The Message of Mission

We have explored the march of mission across continents and through centuries. Now we turn to the message of mission. Is it the same today as it was in the first century? Has it been changed as it was taken to other cultures over the centuries? The church and the person of faith would say no. The message is still Christ and the kingdom of God He proclaimed. The message is still Jesus' redeeming death on the cross and His victory over death in resurrection. The message is still grace, faith, hope, and love.

Historical differences in mission could imply the message is many faceted. As the church has struggled with its mission over the years in different environments and against different challenges, the emphasis of the message seems to have taken different turns.

Trials and Error

In the period from the Great Commission until the triumph of Christian forces in the reign of Constantine in 312, the message of mission seemed to have several emphases.

Kingdom of God

In Christ's lifetime, the message was the announcement of the kingdom of God. In Christ the kingdom had come and it was open to all. Christ announced it to the Jews first in response to the covenant relationship they had with God but quickly made it evident that it embraced all people. His disciples were to enter into the discipline of the rule of God in their hearts and lives. His own death and resurrection would make their entrance possible.

There has been a resurgence in recent years of emphasis on the kingdom of God. In *Mission Between the Times,* C. René Padilla says,

> Salvation is not exclusively forgiveness of sins; it also involved deliverance from the dominion of darkness to a realm in which Jesus is recognized as *Kyrios* of all the universe—the Kingdom of God's beloved Son (Col 1:13).[1]

But some authors feel that this emphasis on the kingdom of God at the heart of the message of mission takes away from the personal evangelistic equation by which each person must come to Christ. Yet the announcement of the kingdom of God coming in Christ was the key transition from the preparatory period that Judaism represented to its fulfillment in Christ and the new covenant which He announced.

> To proclaim the Gospel is to proclaim the message of a Kingdom that is not of this world. The politics of which cannot for that reason conform to the politics of the kingdoms of this world. This is a kingdom whose sovereign rejected "the kingdoms of the world and their glory" in order to establish His own Kingdom on the basis of love. It is a kingdom that is made present among men here and now (Matt. 12:28) in the person of one who does not come from this world (tou cosmou toutou) but "from above" from an order beyond the transitory scene of human existence.[2]

Yet, the basic message of Jesus' mission, the central theme of His preaching, was not the hope of the kingdom coming at some date in the future, but the fact that in His own person and work the kingdom was already present. For this reason many scholars feel Jesus' historical commission can be understood only in terms of the kingdom of God. It was the focus of the initial message of mission.

The New Covenant

The early Christians who shared the contagious word that Christ had risen and that the kingdom had come were doing it in a context of a Judaism that had expected a Messiah but now denied that He had come. Jews who did embrace Christianity were confused by its relationship to their Jewishness. Soon early missionaries were faced with the question of whether non-Jew converts to Christ also had to embrace Judaism. This prompted the great Jerusalem conference detailed in Acts 15. There Paul and Barnabas testified of their experience of preaching the gospel to the Gentiles. This, plus Peter's testimony of his experience with Cornelius, caused the fledgling church to decide not to burden new converts with the requirements of Judaism. It did request that Gentile converts avoid practices that would give offense to their Jewish Christian brethren.

Perhaps no point in the post-Pentecost period of the early church was more critical than this one. The gospel, indeed, was a new covenant and while the old covenant had prepared the way and helped usher it in, the message of mission now stood on new ground fashioned by the Christ, the Son of God.

Ultimate Revelation

A third major emphasis in the message of mission occurred during the apostolic period as the church actually experienced mission in a world of pluralism. This situation is powerfully dramatized in Paul's experience at Athens as he preached at the Areopagus (Acts 17:22 *ff.*).

Paul was deeply involved in preaching the gospel in the

Graeco-Roman world. He taught that the religious dimensions that were present in the lives of all persons were planted there by God as a hunger for His ultimate revelation (that is, Jesus Christ). Paul later spelled out this general revelation in the first chapter of Romans.

But at Athens, Paul referred to the various statues to the gods that the Greeks worshiped as an introduction to the assertion that God had given Jesus Christ to human beings hungering for ultimate reality.

This approach gave Paul an entreé to all people everywhere with the gospel. He had begun with the Jews in each town by preaching that the Messiah for whom they had looked so long and who was foretold in the prophets had come in Jesus Christ. Paul could look to any religious group anywhere and say that the God that they had hungered for and worshiped in such imperfect ways had revealed Himself perfectly in Jesus Christ.

Many African and Asian theologians today who realize that people have come from primitive animism or ancient religions claim that the gospel should be preached to them just as it was preached to the Jews (that is, that Christ was a fulfillment of their religious hunger and their religious background and not a rejection of it). For other Christians this negates the call to "turn from their wicked ways" or focus on the repentance of unbelief. But the thrust of mission in a world of pluralism to see Christ as a fulfillment of hopes existent in all religions is a compelling one. This gave Paul a breakthrough in his desire to find a way to introduce the gospel to the Greek intellectuals at Athens.

Triumph and Tragedy

The period that followed the legitimization of Christianity with the conversion of Constantine is one of both triumph and tragedy. The history of the mission of the church from

312 to 1000 is one of rapid growth. Its ability to come out from the catacombs and be recognized as a legitimate religious expression soon made it dominant in the Roman Empire. Yet it also suffered major problems from the influx of people who were baptized but not "evangelized."

Sign of the Cross

Tradition says that when Constantine was converted he saw a vision in the sky of the cross and the words, "By this sign conquer."

Constantine took the sign of the cross east to establish his new capital in Constantinople in 330. He established the foundation for the Byzantine Empire which would play a significant role in the division of Christianity between East and West. As succeeding emperors placed themselves on the side of Christianity, the sign of the cross seemed to lead the way as a message of mission. Unfortunately the message of mission in this period was often little more than a sign and was used to subjugate people to the faith rather than to persuade them to convert willingly before the thrill of the good news.

Controversy and Creeds

Most historians agree that the early Christians were very missionary in their lives. However, they often worked one-to-one and were low-keyed in the expression of their Christianity because of the tremendous opposition that emerged again and again, first from the Jews and later from the Romans. The church that flourished in the two centuries after the apostolic era often did so underground. The Scriptures that would become the New Testament were still being gathered. Not surprisingly then, during this period differing views about the person of Christ surfaced. Resolving these differences involved consolidations of power and influence, as well as words and creeds.

Beliefs held by Arius and Athanasius polarized the discussion about Christ's humanity and divinity. Arius claimed Christ was "begotten" of God and not coequal. He felt a total equality concept compromised monotheism. Athanasius believed that Christ was coequal with God. At a council called by Constantine in 325 at Nicea, the view that Christ was coequal prevailed and the followers of Arius were banished.[3] Followers of Arius and Anthanasius became ardent missioners, proclaiming their views of the person of Christ, and often became bitter enemies. The politicizing that went with such controversies reflected poorly on all parties.

Monasticism

The more corrupt Christianity became under its highly politicized message, the more genuine Christians sought to recover the purity of the faith and retreat from the discord and corruption. Christian hermits developed monastic retreats from which many missioners emerged with a new focus on the inner life. This focus brought a return to the person of Christ and to the mystic elements of the Christian faith. The message was both inner oriented and service oriented. It persisted as one of the dominant messages of mission until the Reformation and was a part of the forces that brought about the Reformation.

Ecclesiastical

After the fall of Rome and the division of Christian influences into East and West, Western Christianity, freed from state domination, began to assert itself. Christian mission became increasingly ecclesiastical in nature. Being brought into the church was the essence of salvation, and the mission message, rather than receiving Christ or accepting the discipline of His reign. The church of Rome became dominant, and later began to exert its dominance by the threat of excommunication for dissidents. The message of the mission became increasingly clear: Accept the church's authority or suffer damnation. Many students of missions have felt that the ecclesiastical message has dominated Roman Catholic missions and explains something of the problems in Latin America over the years where that message was triumphant.

The Message of the Sword

The period of triumph and tragedy from Constantine through the Crusades was the rickety bridge between the dedicated early church and the institutionalized and politicized church of the Dark Ages.

The period from 1000 to 1200 introduced a new message. The message was a sword. Its showcase was the Crusades. In one sense the Crusades were an understandable response to the Muslim threat to conquer all of Europe in the seventh century. Some Christians strongly endeavored to preach a message of grace and love as an antidote to militant Islam. Far more Christians wanted to reply with equal militarism. They became dominant. At times the sword was used indiscriminately against women and children, and the memory occupies a bitter place in the minds of Muslims. It helps make them the most difficult people with whom to engage in mission to this day.

Darkness and Light

The period from 1200 to 1500 that followed the Crusades was one of darkness for Christianity in many ways. Great missionary efforts had been carried on under one or the other of the mission message themes through the first millennium. But following the Crusades, missions seemed to emerge only from little centers of light in the midst of a larger environment of darkness. Christianity was the tool of political forces and despots who emerged and disappeared through the centuries.

But there were glimmers of light in this period. An example is the preaching of Peter Waldo in the 1200s. Waldo was wealthy merchant of Lyons who became enamored with Christ's message to the rich young ruler. He gave away everything he had and became an itinerant preacher, imitating Christ even in dress and life-style. Waldo was a product of the same spirit that produced Francis of Assisi during the same period. Because Waldo emphasized that Mary was the mother of Christ and not the mother of God, he quickly encountered papal opposition. The Waldensees especially opposed the ecclesiastical message and tried to hold up a simple Christian message and life-style as the solution to church corruption. Heavily persecuted, the Waldensees were nevertheless a vibrant mission force during the Middle Ages.

Reform and Reaction

The Reformation which had roots throughout this period broke into full force in the person of Martin Luther in Germany in the 1500s. His followers and detractors raged back and forth until 1685. Luther's study of the Book of Romans led him to declare that Christ was received "by faith alone." He saw the burden of the ecclesiastical message as the equivalent of the burden of the law that the early church had rejected at the Jerusalem Conference. The Reformation initially did not include a mission emphasis. By freeing the message of mission from ecclesiastical burdens, the Reformation emphasis of grace through faith became the dominant message of mission in the centuries that followed.

But the message of mission that was "by faith alone" spawned reaction that become a message for mission also. The Counter-Reformation mounted by Roman Catholicism focused anew on the ecclesiastical message. In its zeal to win back territory from the Reformers, it captured new territories and developed a dramatic mission effort that spilled into the New World and was most successful in Latin America. The Counter-Reformation also witnessed the formation of the Society of Jesus (the Jesuit order) in 1533 through the efforts of Ignatius Loyola. Ruthless in their opposition to Protestants, they became Roman Catholics' most avid missionaries. Their message was the claims of the Roman Catholic Church.

Message and Message

The period that followed the post-Reformation, from 1685 into the modern age, is one which has seen several messages emerge in the course of the church's affirmation of its mission. In a sense each is a facet of a deeper truth common to all. In another sense the differences are a world map to the problems of the church's mission in this modern period.

Proclamation and Persuasion

Many people feel that the Reformation's recovery of a gospel of grace and faith was a recovery of the concept of proclamation and persuasion as the method of mission. To proclaim that Christ has brought the kingdom of God and to persuade people to receive Christ into their lives along with His forgiveness and the promise of eternal life flowered in the post-Reformation period. As the forerunners of modern denominations emerged, they were preoccupied with declaring the differences that justified their particular expression of faith and with proclaiming and persuading people to embrace Christ.

The Denomination Message

Unfortunately the message of mission in this period often became clouded by denominational differences. From a purely historical point of view, this was not all bad, however, as each different denomination developed its own kind of missionary zeal. Though the denominations often focused on their differences, they did preach Christ. This is especially evident in the message of mission in China and Africa during the great century of missionary advance in the 1800s.

The Ecumenical Message

The mission field, on the other hand, brought out such sharp differences between belief and unbelief that the differences between believers become less compelling and more of an offense to the people being reached in mission. Missionaries longed to downgrade those differences and focus on a simple message of faith. The ecumenical movement emerged out of this longing. Many church groups, and especially missionary centers, tried to get together and focus on a common theme. "Jesus is Lord" became the focus of the ecumenical movement. Yet many strong mission centers, and especially evangelical groups, felt that ecumenical advocates had watered down the gospel to little more than a theme.

The Modern Message

This was also a period of rampant religious rationalism in Europe. Biblical criticism was a topic wherever Christian scholars gathered. One of the aftermaths of this was a downgrading of the conversion element of the message in favor of a focus upon the ethics and morality of the Christian experience as the heart of the message. This further divided missionary groups and led some to lose their mission impetus,

even as others who focused on the more traditional proclamation and persuasion message redoubled their efforts.

Propositional Message

Evangelicals have been accused by some theologians as
resorting to a new form of legalism in the message of mission.
Many Christian thinkers felt that breaking salvation into
"easy" steps was as simplistic and crippling as the proclaim-
ers of the ecumenical message had been in their effort to find
a common denominator.

Liberation Theology

Meanwhile revolution was dominant in the Third World.
Revolutionaries who embraced the faith began to develop a
message of mission around their political aspirations. Liberation theology emerged in Latin America as an approach to
the gospel that preached social and political change more
than individual response. This message of mission is most
evident in centers where East clashes with West and where
Communism and democracy interface. It especially
flourishes where the difference between "have" and "have-
nots" has become intolerable to the masses. While traditional
Christians have tried to learn something from this message,
they have been increasingly convinced that it is a departure
from the real message of mission.

The Abiding Core

Throughout the march of mission in history, the message
of mission has had an abiding core, however. The kingdom
of God that Christ proclaimed has not been lost to the heart
of believers in every age. Despite excesses and departures
from the normal message, men and women of goodwill and
the simple faith that God was in Christ reconciling the world
unto Himself have kept the message of mission alive and,

thus, have kept the mission itself alive. The mission of the church has burned brightly in the midst of almost every turn the church has taken and in the midst of every era that it has passed through.

The abiding core is at the heart of both the proclamation and persuasion and the ecclesiastical message. It undergirds liberation theologies, and it asserts itself in modernism. This is not a way of saying everybody is right, but it does say that what is right refuses to be squelched under any condition. More, it says the gospel has made itself relevant to all conditions. According to Albert McClellan, "The message of the church is timeless, but its presentation must be timely. Churches must emphasize their constants, common both to the day of the New Testament and the day of Satellites and super bombs."[4]

Notes

1. C. René Padilla, *Mission Between the Times* (Grand Rapids, Mich.; William B. Eerdmans Publishing Company, 1985), p. 27.

2. Ibid, p. 4.

3. Kenneth Scott Latourette, *A History of Christianity*, pp. 153 *ff*.

4. Albert McClellan, *The Mission Task of Church*, p. 5.

5

The Method of Mission

Despite its title this chapter does not constitute a "how-to" chapter for a church grappling with its mission in the more practical sense of the word. The "Popular Mechanics" approach to methods is being explored in a lot of areas, but the church seems to respond best to the simple example of the one who gave it its mission. Methods are both inherent in the church's commission and acted out in the life of Jesus Christ. In Matthew 4:23, for instance, the Scripture says that "he went about all Galilee, teaching in their synagogues and preaching the gospel of the kingdom, and healing every disease and every infirmity among the people." On this point, René Padilla claimed,

> Together with the kerygma with the diaconia and the didache, this presupposes a concept of salvation that included the whole man and cannot be reduced to the simple forgiveness of sins and assurance of an unending life with God in Heaven. A comprehensive mission corresponds to a comprehensive view of salvation. Salvation is wholeness. Salvation is total humanization. Salvation is eternal life, the life of the Kingdom of God, life that begins here and now.[1]

This means the ministry of Jesus that we are called to emulate ("as my Father hath sent me, so send I you," John 20:21, KJV) involves proclaiming the gospel, teaching the implications of that gospel, and ministering to all manner of hurt and need.

Bill Austin noted:

> Jesus' activities consisted basically of a preaching-teaching and caring-healing ministry. The former involved the content of his message and the latter the authority of his person.[2]

The Great Commission specifically focuses on making disciples and teaching them all things. This seems to stress preaching and teaching and only imply ministering. Yet from the beginning, the church expressed its mission as Christ did—in proclamation, teaching, and ministry in response to human need and Christian compassion.

A study of methods then, will deal first with the example of Jesus, which we shall call incarnational and which will include proclamation, teaching, and ministry. The study will then focus on the vital connections which have enabled such efforts through the centuries. The strategies that such connections have followed in carrying out missions becomes the overview, thus taking the study from the smallest to the largest.

Incarnational

The term *incarnate* means "to become flesh." The advent of Christ means that the "Word became flesh" as the Gospel of John so eloquently states (1:14). In Christ's life the church received its mission and saw it exemplified.

Proclamation

Christ's earthly ministry began with proclamation. Christ proclaimed the kingdom of God first and foremost. He proclaimed what that kingdom would mean to people. Deliverance and new relationships would emerge. This proclamation calls people to embrace its discipline. That is the heart of making disciples.

But this proclamation also involves what the theologians have called the "kerygma" or the content of the good news that Jesus Christ spelled out in His words and in His life, death, and resurrection.

Jesus himself did not put a tremendous emphasis in the kerygma on salvation from sin but that implication became one of the most hungered for dimensions of the gospel as it was preached from Christ's announcement of the kingdom onward. That men have a sense of sin and that their transgressions weigh heavily upon them is a fact of every culture and all history. That hearts can be hardened and conciousness dulled is documented by evil and violence among all people. But a hunger for cleansing and redemption seems to lay dormant in the breast of every race and responds dramatically to the good news when it comes.

Whether the deep hunger for salvation from sin excites more response than the concept of eternal life that Christ preached may be like arguing two sides of the same coin. But the fact that death is not the final victor over life is undoubtedly one of the gemstones of the kerygma.

While the Egyptians buried their kings with paraphernalia for opulence in the next world on one continent, nomadic tribes on another buried their dead with the simple instruments they would need to cope with another life envisioned very much as the one they had just left. People from all cultures and all ages have hungered to transcend the brevity of life, its often untimely cessation, and the myriads of threats to it that seem to dominate the horizon whether from the violence of other men, the whims of nature, or the mysteries of disease.

Christ's proclamation of good news stood out above even the drama of His miracles. "Did not our hearts burn within

us while he talked to us . . .?" two followers exclaimed to each
other (Luke 24:32).

Preaching and Witness

Proclamation of the kerygma from the earliest days of the
mission until now has assumed many different forms. In its
simplest form, it is the sharing of the experience of one
person with another. That is still the most powerful form of
communication. Television recognizes this fact with its tes-
timonials. One-on-one selling depends upon one person
sharing with another what something has meant to them.
Philip's simple witness to the Ethiopian eunuch offers an
early illustration of such sharing (see Acts 8:26-40).

But the gospel has a "shout it from the housetops" quality
that amplifies sharing into preaching. Shortly after Pentecost
Peter began speaking to large groups, even as his Master had
done.

Because of the drama of preaching, it has become the focus
for sharing the kerygma. Gifted men and women have delivered their eloquence and powers of public oratory to the
mission of the church again and again. Much of the history
of missions can be written in terms of the effectiveness of
individuals who mounted pulpits, whether those pulpits were
tree stumps in a frontier wilderness or magnificent settings
in lofty cathedrals.

But proclamation involves more than announcing the gospel. It involves the persuading of people to make a commitment to, in fact become disciples of, the Master, to take upon
themselves the discipline of the kingdom of God. People who
do this became radically different. This "conversion"
becomes the score-card of preaching. From the time when
King Agrippa said to Paul, "You almost persuade me" to
now persuasion has become a definite part of proclamation.

On the American frontier open-air preaching was part of

the church's mission. Such preaching was sponsored by congregational groups, such as Methodists, Presbyterians, and Baptists and later the Disciples and Churches of Christ. Great preaching voices called multitudes to repentance and faith in Christ. Examples are George Whitefield, Charles G. Finney, Dwight L. Moody, Billy Sunday, and, in recent years, Billy Graham. Graham, using broadcasting, publications, and effective promotional techniques, has preached to millions on every continent, and though from Presbyterian and Baptist roots, has managed to preach above denominational or sectarian lines.

Publishing

While sharing the kerygma person-to-person in one-on-one situations, in small-groups, or to large crowds became the most obvious way to proclaim the gospel, the task called for ways to reach more people over larger areas and for sustained periods of time. The written word was the obvious answer. Letters from the pen of Paul, accounts of the life of Christ, and epistles from the men who walked with Him or knew those who did were copied and shared. In time the church gathered this material into the canon that became the New Testament. At times only the clergy had access to the Bible or had the education to read it. Whenever the laity or common people picked it up, it was often a source of tension and sometimes persecution within the church (see, for example, the stories of John Huss and John Knox).

But from the very first, writing, tracts, and books became a vital part of the proclamation of the kerygma. Church history categorizes early Christian writings in terms of polemics (those that argued for the faith), apologetics (those that interpreted the faith), and catechisms (simple teaching tools). Monasteries provided a base for the circulation of such documents. They were gathered in libraries and laboriously copied.

The invention of the painting press in the early Renaissance dramatically changed the world. The written word could be spread on a scale beyond anybody's imagination. The impact of reading the Scriptures could be experienced by more individuals.

In later years, small pamphlets or tracts became the staple of mass proclamation. Missionaries who had not yet mastered a new language could communicate effectively through such tracts. In areas where no written language existed, men and women labored for years and suffered great privations to make a written word possible. One of the largest missionary organizations in the world, the Wycliffe Bible Translators, is dedicated to this task.[3] Publishing houses have become standard operating procedure for Christian missions in every land.

Broadcasting

The next great revolution in proclaiming the kerygma could not have been comprehended by the early church. Even as the printing press took the written word into dimensions that they did not dream of, broadcasting took it into a world they had no reason to believe existed.

Broadcasting refers, first of all, to radio. The Marconi experiments, which allowed the voice of one person to be received in distant places, revolutionized proclamation. While it can be argued that the telegraph and the telephone provided one-on-one possibilities, the radio opened up the voice of witness, testimony, proclamation, and persuasion to multitudes beyond the local scene.

Missionary radio is said to have begun on Christmas Day 1931 with the first broadcast of station HCJB in Quito, Ecuador. According to J. Herbert Kane, sixty-five such stations existed by 1983, not to mention thousands of Christian programs beamed over commercial stations each year around the world. Citing the Far Eastern Broadcasting Company of Manila as an example, Kane said that this group has twenty-eight transmitters airing nineteen hundred hours a week in ninety-one languages and dialects on three continents. Is anyone listening? According to Kane, FEBC receives over thirty thousand letters a month from over one hundred countries.[4]

Today broadcasting is one of the most effective forms of mission in terms of the number of people who hear the message. Gigantic antennas such as those of FEBC beam gospel messages and gospel teaching around the world. Of course, radios and televisions are necessary for the message to be received. In mission settings, a few hundred people might tune in to a program and a still smaller group might have understood the message. But missionaries in one place have been able to reach many people through broadcasting.

Currently television has become the focus of kerygma broadcasting in more advanced countries. Local churches often use television to open the windows and doors of worship experiences to people throughout a community. The network evangelists of our time have shown how effective television can become and how many people it can reach.

Of course, this has brought new problems of competing messages, financial exploitation, and charges of political propaganda. For the mission of the church, however, the reality of broadcasting is the key point.

Teaching

Teaching as an incarnational method of mission is probably the least controversial dimension of mission. The church has always felt that "teaching them to observe all things whatsoever I have taught you" is vital to its mission.

Many Christians believe that proclamation is the planting of the seed and teaching is bringing that seed to fruition. On many mission fields, converts cannot be baptized until they have been through a period of teaching and can demonstrate that they understand not only the gospel but how they should live the demands of the gospel.

In early days teachers were the key to the advance of the church. New converts traveled hundreds of miles to live with gifted and wise teachers and learn from them. Mentoring became one of the most effective forms of teaching. The focus of teaching from the beginning has been in the church. At no point has the mission of the church been more significantly expressed in terms of the church as an institution than in teaching. The early church undertook, as the synagogue had before, the task of the systematic teaching of what Christ had taught and the Christian concepts that proliferated around His teachings.

The monasteries that developed during the Middle Ages became centers for education and mission. This coincided with the gathering of literature already mentioned. The earliest Gospels and New Testament letters were gathered in the monasteries. They, in turn, became the curriculum for Christian leadership and especially the clergy that led the medieval church.

The monasteries gave way to informal schools and these schools, in turn, to more formal institutions of learning that gave rise to the modern university. Initially, universities were a focus and a function of the mission of the church. The secularization of many came quickly, however. The seed of their secularization were probably sown in their founding through the role of the Renaissance. Fortunately many smaller institutions continue to serve the Christian roles for which they were founded.

One of the most important things about the teaching role

in the mission of the church is that teaching centers have strongly influenced the directions taken by the church.

As the earliest universities became secularized, churches established new ones dedicated to training both for the marketplace and to open the world of knowledge around the integrating concept of Christ. A more direct legacy of the monasteries and the teaching task has been seminaries. The seminaries focused on training people specifically for leadership in the churches.

Publishing also has become critical in the on-going teaching task. Publishing houses sponsored by churches, denominations, and Christian societies have been at the heart of the modern teaching efforts of the mission of the church.

Sunday Schools, which become an institutional form of regular teaching, did not emerge until the 1800s in England and the United States and then followed the church's strong missionary outreach around the world.

As the mission has penetrated new fields with the gospel over the years, it has depended heavily on the establishment of institutions with a teaching focus to develop the field. Therefore, every country where Christian mission has flourished has generally sprouted schools, colleges, training centers, and seminaries.

Conflict

But the teaching task of the church's mission has been the source of much conflict. Teaching too often focused on the denominational distinctives that set it off from another group of Christians. Or it focused on methods for practicing its brand of the faith rather than sharing the implications of the faith. It has been the teaching task more than the proclamation task that has become the seedbed for so many of the differences, distinctions, and disturbances in the Christian fellowship. Even today, as the gospel struggles with questions of equality, political freedom, poverty, race, and peace, the church's teaching mission reacts in different ways.

When Christ in the Great Commission commanded His followers to teach all things that He had shared with them, He not only wanted them to understand the full implications of the gospel but also wanted their lives to reflect the true disciplines of the reality of the kingdom. Liberation theology in the Third World may look like a political mutation of the real gospel, but it is an understandable result based on what Jesus taught and preached about delivering the oppressed and the needs of the poor. That women's roles, racial issues, and concern about health and opportunity should ultimately be included in such teaching is inherent in the nature of the gospel.

Ministry

Jesus' earliest example, however, focused as much on acts of care and compassion as it did on proclamation and teaching. The Gospels record the feeding of the multitudes, the healing of the sick, and stories of caring for widows and orphans, the hungry and the naked, and the jailed and oppressed.

Healing

Inspired by Jesus' example, His followers have attempted to minister to those in need around them. As part of the mission of the church, men and women have plunged into the most dangerous situations and laid down their lives to minister for a brief time to suffering humanity. Dedicated followers of Jesus Christ have penetrated jungles, crossed oceans, and climbed mountains to bring healing to fellow human beings in the name of Jesus Christ.

In the early years of Christian history, plague-racked cities found only Christians willing to collect the bodies that harbored the disease. For years only Christian missioners could be counted on to reach out to the lepers of this world.

While in our time we have recognized that such a spirit can draw its impetus from other religious dimensions or from no religion at all, one invariably finds Christian roots in the beliefs that fuel such ministries.

Because of this, Christian mission hospitals came into being. Medical missions was in the forefront in the great advance of missions in the nineteenth and twentieth centuries. Some people have credited Christian medicine with opening certain territories, such as China, when preachers or teachers could not.

As responsibility for health care was picked up by the state, however, more and more medical missionaries had to turn their tasks over to nationals who were in it as professionals and not as a Christian ministry. Christian clinics and hospitals remain, however, and continue to be at the forefront of Christian mission.

Hunger

Even as Jesus fed the five thousand, so Christians have been called to share with the hungry of the world. In the earliest days, Paul led churches to gather supplies and monies to help take care of people in less fortunate areas. Famine has been a persistent reality in the world to this very day. Christian mission forces have gone to great lengths to help wherever it emerges. In 1986 church mission groups were very evident in dealing with rampant starvation in the Sudan.

Church agricultural technicians have gone to various parts of the world to try to alleviate recurring famine by sharing advanced agricultural techniques with people who have been trapped in cycles that give no relief from the vagaries of weather patterns and worn-out soils.

Many Christians in the United States have been very active in agricultural politics, not for political reasons but because they believe there is enough food in the world to penetrate pockets of famine everywhere. Television provides graphic pictures of the ravages of famine: pot-bellied children, decimated young men and women, and retarded people who lack the foodstuffs that in places like America exist in abundance.

Relief

The mission of responding to people in Christlike ways has led Christians to join relief efforts into many war-torn situations. Christians have delivered clothes, blankets, medical supplies and foodstuffs. The first aid to many disaster victims has come from Christians.

In Mexico City in 1984 a devastating earthquake caused thousands of deaths. Christian churches from America responded immediately and, many felt, more effectively than much larger bureaucratic enterprises. While the latter soon took over the task, the people involved will not forget the impact of help coming in the name of Jesus Christ.

Vocational

Many mission efforts have included Christian training centers to help people care for themselves. The establishment of churches is greatly helped in new areas when believers can provide for their own living and pick up the task of mission themselves.

Summary

That the methods of missions still focus on the life of Christ and His example of proclamation, teaching, and ministry is obvious. The sophistications and technologies of our age have multiplied the expressions of these methods of mission, but they have not basically changed them. When a local church sharply senses its mission, it inevitably begins to express it in such forms.

Connectional

The word *connectional* refers in the simplest sense to the gathering of believers in the local fellowship we call a church. That gathering is so vital the New Testament often refers to it as a body. Each such body is a part of the larger church and the church is, of course, part of the kingdom of God. But connectionalism in the sense that it is used here refers to Christians connecting either as individuals from differing fellowships in a specific alliance for mission or through churches pooling their resources through boards or agencies for mission. The goal, of course, in this key method of mission is to make larger resources available to develop a larger impact on the massive task.

Church Centers

At Jerusalem and Antioch, believers may have met in more than one fellowship but considered themselves as a single church even as some Pentecostal churches are beginning to do in places like Argentina and Korea.[5] These local church centers became the earliest forms of connection for missionary outreach. The first such outreach recorded in Scripture involved the sending of Paul and Barnabas from Antioch. Later, as the church in Jerusalem endeavored to resolve some of the questions that emerged in the mission task, it also became involved as a sending body.

These urban churches became centers of mission activity during the first centuries of the march of mission. As smaller churches became dependent upon larger ones, the earliest connectional tactics developed.

State-Church Centers

After Christianity became a legal religion and enjoyed the blessings of the state, churches were quick to employ the power of the state in carrying out its mission. Often a Christian monarch encouraged the sending of missionaries or the reaching out with mission intent. This happened in a negative way in the Crusades but in a more positive way in the missions to England and the European Low Countries.

Monastic Centers

Monastic centers soon rivaled the state as a major form of connection for the mission task. With patronage from wealthy landowners or from heads of states, many monasteries gathered enough wealth and personnel to carry out significant missions. In the Protestant Reformation, universities became connectional bases for mission.

Societal

The societal connection had its roots in the great Roman Catholic brotherhoods, such as those gathered by Francis of Assisi and Ignatius Loyola. The Franciscans and the Jesuits certainly did not encompass all of the Roman Catholic missionary thrust, but they became a potent example of connectional effectiveness in focusing the resources of many believers and the wealth of many churches on the mission task.

In the modern mission movement, societies such as England's Society for the Propagation of the Gospel in New England and the Society for Promoting Christian Knowledge, the Society for the Propagation of the Gospel in Foreign Parts, and later the Church Missionary Society showed the booming nature of this form of connectionalism among Protestants. In the United States, the earliest missionary groups were societal, such as the Baptists who organized to back Adoniram and Ann Judson and Luther Rice when they rejected their Congregational roots. More recently single-thrust societies, such as the Wycliffe Translators, the Missionary Aviation Fellowship, and New Tribes Missions, show that the societal forms of connection for gathering believers' efforts in mission is still alive and well.

Denominational

The denominational form of connectionalism has probably been the most powerful force in Christian mission to this date. While Roman Catholicism and its collective forms would numerically be the largest, from a Protestant point of view, denominational missions led the great century of advance. That they still are a force to be reckoned with is typified by the Southern Baptist Convention's Foreign Mission Board, the largest of the denominational endeavors and the largest missionary force currently among Protestants.

The Anglicans supported both societies and denominational connections. The Methodist, Presbyterians, Congregationalists, and Baptists became the most adept at connecting their resources as denominations and launching strong missionary efforts throughout the world.

Implications

Believers and churches everywhere grapple with the biblical reality of their mission and its implications for their lives. One person can do some things and one church can do more. Churches and believers who connect with others for the task have made the major differences through the years.

A sense of mission absolutely demands a healthy connection for its task. It not only ties together institutions of education and training with those of mission efforts, but it provides facilitating resources for penetrating and sustaining new areas. Only strong connections can develop the strategies and assemble the resources necessary to make major differences in the spreading of the gospel.

Strategical

The mission of the church from the earliest days has reflected an expansionary dimension explicit in the Great Commission. The gospel was to be preached in ever-expanding circles that reached from Jerusalem to the ends of the world and from that time to the end of the age. Though the focus was not on numbers, the emphasis inevitable was.

Church Planting

The initial focus of the church had to do with the church in its broadest or spiritual sense (that is, "The gates of hell shall not prevail against it."). But when it found definite expressions in places like Antioch, Ephesus, Corinth, and Rome, the role of the local church came into its own. Paul's mission strategy focused on gathering believers into local fellowships who understood themselves to be church in every sense of the word. The church found that the best way to make disciples, baptize, and teach was to reproduce itself, to plant new churches among new peoples and in new locales. These churches, in turn, became centers for reaching others with the gospel.

Talmadge Amberson said it's when "we look at what actually happened in the New Testament that lends support to the planting of churches."[6] He pointed out that the New Testament itself does not command us to plant churches, but rather to preach the gospel. The gospel, in turn, breeds churches. The church becomes the result of mission and then the church becomes the focus of continuing that mission.

Church planting through the years has been at the heart of all Christian mission. When it was not explicit, it was implicit as believers emerged from preaching or as they were gathered by circumstances that drew them together or as they were singled out in the midst of large populations and forced together because of what they had in common. But they became churches, and as churches they recognized and responded to their mission.

Territorial

The initial focus of Christian mission, however, was not on planting churches but on preaching the gospel everywhere. The Great Commission is territorial. And territories drew the Christian mission on its way. Roman roads led from place to place and were followed in the course of commerce and trade. Even persecution moved believers into new territories. The Roman world that was part of the "fulness of time" discussed earlier allowed the initial territorial impetus of the Christian mission to focus around the Mediterranean Sea in Egypt, North Africa, and Asia Minor, all Roman territories.

Tradition holds that missions moved as far east as India, as far south as Ethiopia, and as far north as England as early as the first century.

In the middle years of the march of missions, the territorial task was more of a natural bleeding over into the next frontier than it was a specific march to a new territory to plant churches or preach the gospel.

But the modern reader must remember the maps of the world in those days. Marco Polo's adventures were largely unheard of. Western expansion was still limited by the concept of a flat earth and unknown horrors. Territories were thought of in terms of uneasy lines of truce between identified states. It remained for the more modern missionary movement led by colonialism in many forms to make the territorial method of missionary expansion truly operative. During this period, planting the gospel in such places as the "dark continent" of Africa became an imperative. Penetrating the Roman Catholic bastion of Latin America by Protestant missionary forces became irresistible. Establishing the gospel in the ancient kingdoms of China and Japan drew mission-minded people and galvanized the efforts of mission-minded churches.

As the modern map emerged, mission imperatives drew dedicated fingers across the symbols of oceans, rivers, and mountains to pinpoint frontiers for new missionary enter-prises. The territorial strategy became dominant.

At one mission board new maps are published each time a missionary from that board is located in a new country. Such countries are colored a distinctive hue. Thus, as each new map emerges, the territorial progress of that board's mission is graphically displayed. A number of years ago, one of its executives spoke of a couple newly located in Botswana. He reported they were still in a hotel, unable to find a place to live. They could not speak one word of the language, and they were beset by dysentery and other problems while trying to adapt to the local foodstuffs. They had not won one con-vert but the board published a new map and colored the country occupied.

The territorial appeal has drawn Christians and galvan-ized churches for two centuries now with obvious effective-ness. Primarily tied to the church-planting concept, the territorial method continues to challenge Christian churches in their mission.

Demographic

Another strategy has involved following particular people. Called the demographic strategy, it is in one sense the line of least resistance. The strategy follows the gospel through a family or a tribe, or a language group, no matter to what territory that might lead. Obviously, Paul pioneered this method when he went from synagogue to synagogue in the mission to Asia Minor.

One of the early illustrations in this book told of the mission advance in East Africa among the Giryama people. This is a prime example of the demographic method. It can also become a limiting factor when people are reluctant to leave the boundaries of language groups where they can be understood and cultures where they can readily recognize the rules of acceptable living.

But since the mission of the church constantly calls people to cross such boundaries, many of the mission strategies of the past two centuries have focused on particular groups of people rather than territories. Missions that have focused upon language, such as the Wycliffe Translators and the New Tribes Missions, are examples of mission efforts to follow particular peoples wherever they are found.

Adapting the church to individual cultures has been a problem through the centuries. In modern missions, it has been more obvious in places like Africa where tribal customs were often ignored and church growth was limited. More than one missionary observed that *Robert's Rules of Order* prevailed over the natural development of the gospel.

Leadership forms imported from the West often failed to come to grips with the unique dimensions of a particular culture or people, and only in recent years have people begun to analyze how churches grow in different demographic situations (that is in different cultural or people group situations).

Thus, while demographic strategies like territorial strategies grew up as natural avenues of Christian mission, they have become specific strategies of those committed to Christian mission.

Urban

From the very beginning of the church's mission, it found itself working in urban centers. Churches quickly appeared in Jerusalem, Antioch, Ephesus, and Rome. Commerce and travel made cities natural places for churches to gather. Urban strategies, therefore, initially were more incidental to the task of mission than they were primary. Later they became primary extensions of territorial and demographic methods.

But as the march of mission moved on, the gospel often prospered most in rural areas. The rural areas became the line of least resistance and while the large church centers in urban areas were the ones that drew attention, in the rural areas lives were most profoundly affected and societies most completely ordered around the gospel.

On the American frontier, for instance, evangelistic efforts found their most fertile fields in smaller towns and rural areas rather than large urban centers. One reason might have been that rural areas constituted homogenous units, a kind of demographic opportunity.

But the world is increasingly being urbanized as David Barrett has chronicled so minutely in his *Encyclopedia of Christian Missions.*

In a work that is almost an abstract, *World-Class Cities and World Evangelism,* Barrett reviews the history of the church in urban areas and shows that the church gained dramatically in key urban areas from 1800 to 1900 but, in the twentieth century, has lost ground just as dramatically. He wrote of mega-cities, supercities, and supergiants and challenged Christian churches toward a new mission to such urban centers.

The problem is that urban areas used to facilitate mission by presenting great concentrations of peoples that provided miniterritorial and demographic opportunities. Now, with giant highrises standing like armed fortresses, with people isolated and fearful of one another, urban areas are more often barriers to a compelling witness and efforts to plant new churches. In part, this is one reason broadcasting, and especially television, activities have become so important in modern missions. But it is also a reason that the nurturing and planting of churches is so much more critical now.

Barrett has put the urban phenomena in sharp contrast with a chronology of urban missions.[8]

1. Background: The origins of urbanization (8900 BC: city of Jericho)

2. God's self-revelation begins, linked with cities (1950 BC: Ur of the Chaldees; call of Abram)

3. Birth of Christianity as an urban phenomenon (AD 33: Jerusalem; Pentecost regarded as urban missions outreach)

4. Christianity becomes organized with metropolitian structures (AD 249: Paris)

5. The Dark Ages: Decline of cities and urban Christendom (AD 500; sack of Rome)

6. Protestant Reformation spreads via German and Swiss cities (AD 1517: city of Wittenberg)

7. Modern missionary movement emphasizes urban ministry (AD 1705: city of Halle)

8. Large-scale urban team evangelism begins (AD 1857: Chicago)

9. New types of urban missions emerge: radio, television, *et al.* (AD 1921: Pittsburg)

10. Global international mass evangelism develops (AD 1907: Amsterdam)

Many people, including Barrett, see urban strategies as the key to the church's mission in the years immediately ahead and urban centers themselves the future of world history.

Summary

The mission strategies of church planting, territorial out-reach, demographic expansion, and urban outreach may not offer a local church much more than a sense of history and perhaps an overwhelming awareness of the task remaining. But the local church must grapple with the growing size of the task not from an individual point of view but from a connectional point of view.

Conclusion

The church must recover an awareness of biblical methods that it might not dissipate itself without the focus and clear-cut example that Jesus Christ gave us. It must be aware that its mission is *everywhere* and that its opportunities are rapid-ly changing. The church especially needs a strong sense of what God has already placed in its hands for the task and the abilities to see the opportunities around it.

Mission is still one believer's response to the discipline of the kingdom of God and the indwelling Spirit of God. But it is also Christians in concert with other Christians. In-dividual churches must understand that there are other churches caught up in mission with whom, in concert, they can enter into the grand plan of God for the ages.

Notes

1. C. René Padilla, *Mission Between the Times* (Grand Rapids, Mich.: William B. Eerdmans Publishing Company, 1985) p. 22.

2. Bill Austin., *Austin's Topical History of Christianity,* p. 33.

3. Founded 1935, the Wycliffe Bible Translators had 4,205 workers in 1981.

4. J. Herbert Kane, *Understanding Christian Missions*, 3rd ed., p. 166.

5. Ibid. p. 16.

6. Talmadge Amberson, comp., *The Birth of Churches*, p. 34.

7. The author to a group of newly appointed missionaries in an orientation seminar at Richmond, Va in 1965.

8. David B. Barrett, *World-Class Cities and World Evangelization*, p. 11.

6
The Mission of the Local Church

Much of the emphasis of this book has been on the larger church that encompasses believers and fellowships of believers everywhere under whatever name. But as has been obvious in almost every phase of this study, one is constantly driven to the local scene, to a local fellowship of believers for the illustrative material. The reason is simple. The mission is ultimately that of a local church.

Recently, in a meeting promoting a mission emphasis in a Southwestern state, an effort was made to raise funds for a bold church-planting effort. A denominational promotional group suggested that fifteen thousand dollars would provide a church. "Give a church" they urged the listeners. While sympathy must be given to the task of fund raising, and some license must be given to metaphors for mission, this approach does violence to basic truths about the local church. A church is not bought nor does it have a price tag. It is the work of God's Spirit in the midst of a localized group of people. Individual believers come together, obviously because they are in the same locale, but, more significantly, because they have recognized in each other a kinship in Christ.

The Bible teaches that the Spirit gathers such fellowships. Indeed, Paul wrote about the church as a functioning body. (See 1 Cor. 12:12 *ff.*). Each member, according to the gifts of the Spirit, has a unique function within the body. This means that the fellowship is gathered dynamically for its task under the headship of Jesus Christ. The church's mission is never more recognizable than it is in a local church's response to this sense of having been called out.

A Sense of Mission

What causes a local church fellowship to have a sense of mission? Without a serious case study of many local churches along a continuum ranging from almost no awareness of mission to an all-encompassing sense of mission, that question probably cannot be answered with scientific accuracy. Perhaps a broader statement leads more nearly to the practical truth. A church develops a sense of mission by being a church. A gathered community of believers worshiping regularly, teaching the Word of God, and ministering to one another invariably senses mission. As it uses the Word of God in worship it encounters again and again the scriptural admonitions that have constituted the commission for the church. It is confronted by the background that shows that the church is a result of God's mission and that in Christ it has inherited His mission. In worship, individuals experience a desire, a drive, to share their joy. Proclamation is not something the church decides to do, but something, being the church, it inevitably does.

Many local churches have found that the way to heighten mission awareness is to begin teaching the Scriptures from the perspective of the mission of the church. Many points of focus can make the Scriptures live for a group of believers, but few are as compelling as this one. Taking the mission of the church as a focus, begin studying any particular passage or book in the Bible and see what happens.

Indeed, the modern mission movement begins with William Carey's study of the Scriptures from the perspective of an expanding world and his questions about the mission of the church.[1]

But the focus can be more personal. A study of what Jesus did during His earthly ministry opens up for the average believer and the average church a world of possibilities amid the life that swarms about them.

Another way to heighten the local church's sense of mission is to expose it to examples of churches that are deeply involved in mission.

Years ago, while pastoring a local church in Tennessee, I shared with a group of church leaders the story of what a church in San Antonio, Texas, had been doing for the poor in their area. After I recounted the story, one of the women in the group said, "Why, we could do that." That example opened up a strategic new ministry for our church.

God's Spirit is at work in the church throughout the world. In any given local congregation, there might be a breakthrough of insights and possibilities yielding new techniques for the task. Sharing this from one church to the next is a challenge. Sharing it across traditional denominational lines is a challenge. Sharing it in a way that can be seen suggestively and not critically may be the greatest challenge of all. Even as an individual can be inspired and motivated to action by the example of another individual, local churches can be inspired and motivated to action by the example of other churches.

But because the church is the people of God and the Spirit of God dwells in their midst, quickening them to the new life they are leading, the most dramatic factor in creating a sense of mission in a local church may be discovering what is going on around them.

Awareness of Strategic Situation

Early in the ministry of King Saul, the prophet Samuel told him to go down the road and put his hand to that which he found to do. (See 1 Sam. 10:7.) In a way this is a local church's admonition. It need not look very far or go very far before it finds much to do. Like the good Samaritan, on its journey the church will find the wounded and bleeding on the side of the road. Like Philip, the church will find an Ethiopian traveler with a hungry heart. Like Paul, it will encounter trembling jailers ready to receive the gospel.

How can a church heighten its awareness of its strategic situation? In one sense the admonition to "lift up your eyes" ought to be enough. But more, the local church that is serious about its sense of mission needs to do a careful analysis of just where it is, just what is happening about it, and just what the Spirit of God would press it to see and do.

W. L. Howse and W. O. Thomason in their book, *A Dynamic Church,* said,

> To engage in mission action, a church must take three essential actions: (a) discover needs for mission action and select from those the needs it will meet, (b) provide opportunities for persons to engage in mission action, and (c) enlist persons in mission action.[2]

Howse and Thomason held that the approaches used by a local church in its community were identical to those used by missionaries throughout the world.

Obviously, if a church is in a rural setting it will be looking at a world of opportunities quite different from those that a suburban church might find or an inner-city church might confront. But no gathered group of believers, from the most remote environment to the most teeming one, is without strategic opportunities to share the gospel. The borders may be placed differently. A church in a less-populous situation might draw its bead on more distant sites. It might have a "going" dimension that has to cover many miles to target situations on which it can bring gospel resources and spiritual light.

On the other hand, a church in an inner-city setting might find it cannot get inside the doors of its place of worship without walking through dozens of mission opportunities. Its mission has come to it. Its strategic situation puts it in the midst of almost more need than it can sort out.

An awareness of such strategic situations, however, needs to be spiritually understood. It is more than a demographic analysis or a needs analysis that United Way might do. It is the study of the situation in light of Jesus Christ and what He is about and what He has given the church to do.

Christians must face some of the same problems that others do, however, when in the midst of overwhelming need. They can develop a disdain for the very people who need them the most. Christian compassion has to rise above such natural responses. It has to reach beyond its own revulsions.

In a local church in Tennessee the pastor realized his staff had come to dislike the task of dealing with the transients who trooped in day after day, asking for help or handouts. He helped them develop a range of responses and then urged them not to judge the worthiness of the seeker. He called it "no-fault" ministry. Freed from the need to judge, the staff began to delight in helping "as unto the Lord."

As the people of a particular fellowship of believers meet, they are usually gathered from a varied set of circumstances. Each has the ability to observe or see things that the others may need to hear about in terms of opportunities to share Christ. Many churches have noticed children's needs or young people's needs and have set out to meet those and found that they result in a great opportunity to reach adults and families. Other churches have found pockets of people oppressed by social or economic circumstances and have set out to champion them. As a result, they open up a world of mission opportunities. Churches setting about to provide for the needs of unfortunates with food, clothing, and shelter have found one of the more obvious ways to minister.

One of the challenges facing the church in any such situation is to share the most important thing it has—the Good News in Jesus Christ. Ministry that does not share its ultimate treasure is not true ministry. It is holding the best back.

At the wedding in Cana the guests were amazed that the best wine came last (the wine that Jesus provided from simple water, see John 2:1 *ff.*). Mission activity that begins with acts of mercy and ministry should yield the good wine of the gospel as opportunity presents itself.

The strategic situation of a local church, however, should not cause the church to develop myopia. It must see past its neighborhood, its locale, and its area to the "global village" that technology and time have made of our world. Only as a local church engages in global outreach does it have a true sense of mission. While this can involve direct actions by a church, more often than not it will provoke a vital exploration of connectional opportunities.

For many churches in strong denominational settings, such as Southern Baptists, their very life came into being around such connectional structures for mission.[3] Southern Baptists began by organizing a foreign mission board and a domestic mission board and came together, in essence, to support those connectional mission activities.

In turn, the outreach that comes with foreign missions, for instance, can sensitize a church to what is going undone at hand. During the days when segregation was breaking down in the United States, mission-minded churches were aware of the contradiction between their approach to people of other races in places like Africa and their approach to blacks in the

United States. More than one church moved from mission mindedness to a local change of attitude.

A church that can develop an awareness of its strategic situation, both locally and globally, will find that its sense of mission not only heightened but also yielding new ways to express itself. When this happens, new awareness of God's working in our midst and its part in the broader purposes of what God is about in our time can be positively invigorating.

Awareness of Gifts and Resources

According to New Testament teaching, a church is not drawn together haphazardly. If it is to be a body under the headship of Jesus Christ, it is carefully equipped by the Spirit. The spiritual arms and hands, legs and feet, eyes and ears for action and communication are present in the church. Often a church's mission excitement develops when individuals in its midst are called to leave that fellowship under a mandate from God to cross some barrier in a missionary endeavor.

A church may discover in its midst someone who has become deeply involved with a local need and find an opportunity to back that individual or to enter into their task with them. In the city where I live, one member of an Episcopal church became very active in developing a hospice ministry to care for the terminally ill. The whole church soon found itself backing the enterprise and engaging in a mission that was all but ignored by the rest of the Christian community.

A church may find that it has other God-given resources. Some churches include members with a great deal of wealth in their fellowship. Often this wealth is gathered and used to build impressive structures or handsome places to worship. How much more impressive it is when such people pool their resources for a strong mission outreach.

When a church is related to global outreach through a

vital mission connection, an awareness of such resources and what they can mean can bring dramatic results. In the early fifties a wealthy businessman in Nashville, Tennessee, became aware of church building needs in Latin America. His fervent response involved his church and even his denomination in a dynamic program to provide worship facilities for small congregations throughout that part of the world.

One church included in its membership a group of talented athletes and several coaches. They heard about the Fellowship of Christian Athletes and organized a chapter in the high schools in their area as a mission outreach.

In other words, God's imperative is that a church develop an awareness of the gifts and resources for mission in its midst. They are part and parcel of its calling.

Nor can a church ignore technical skills under the misconception they are foreign to a spiritual endeavor. Through the years ham radio operators in many congregations have helped fellow church members become directly involved in mission needs around the world and facilitated ministry through the communications they provided. More recently computer buffs have discovered opportunities through networking to relate their skills to their missionary convictions.

Many pilots of small aircraft for years have longed to wed their love for flying and their skill in navigating the airways with their Christian convictions. Some have become a part of a worldwide network providing mission air support called Mission Aviation Fellowship. Local churches have also developed mission airlifts for people needing to get to a hospital from remote areas or people moving between mission points that involve great distances. They have provided transport for needed supplies. One church in the panhandle of Texas has several members with planes that regularly transport other members of its fellowship to the Mexican border in a project called River Missions.

Perhaps bankers or stockbrokers in a church who have skills in financial detail can help struggling families put their resources into more orderly repair. People skilled in personnel placement can help the jobless find work. Skilled nurses can help young mothers in underprivileged areas care more effectively for their children.

The list could go on and on, but I hope the point is clear: A church that would be involved in mission must have a strong awareness of the spiritual gifts and resources within its fellowship. Only then can they be addressed to the needs around it.

Maybe this is simply asking: What needs to be done? What do we have with which to do it?

A Plan of Action

A plan of action can sound too much like the corporate model or the business principles that often seem to stand at odds with the spiritual dimensions that undergird a church's activities. But a mission plan of action, simply stated, is a church's decision to do something about a need with gifts and resources it has in its midst. This decision means that the church is mobilizing its own ranks for mission. Such purposefulness is at the heart of a renewed awareness of what it means to be disciples of Jesus Christ as well as a resolve to get something done. For some churches, the plan can be directed toward a specific need, such as an after-school activities program for children or a food bank for the area hungry. For a church with a truly heightened sense of mission, however, a plan of action will probably be more comprehensive.

Mission plans should include an inventory of the needs in the area and the gifts and resources within the fellowship. It should undoubtedly involve more than one kind of mission or ministry, and it should include a strong commitment to share the good news of Jesus Christ in the midst of whatever is being done.

Such plans should include the connectional opportunities for a local church and a global awareness. A church in Abilene, Texas, sponsored several mission trips to a small town in the heart of Brazil where a missionary with ties to that church was at work. Soon dozens of members of that church's fellowship were involved in direct mission trips.

Another church developed an evangelistic partnership with kindred churches in Australia. Summer vacations were used by many of its members to do house-to-house visitation and witnessing in that country where language is no barrier. All this means that world missions and global outreach can be very direct by local churches.

True, if a local church is a small gathering in the Third World, with members struggling to have enough to eat, it may find that its own mission outreach is extremely limited. But the Lord set down the key principles when He said unto whom much is given, much shall be required. The congregation with tremendous opportunities can satisfy itself with no less. In turn, a congregation with few opportunities will need simply to confront those faithfully.

A plan of action for mission, however bold, must be spiritual. It must be conceived in biblical terms, in incarnational ministries, and developed in a Spirit-led manner. Prayer and supplication go with any mission task.

The church is not of the world. It has been called out of the world though its mission is to the world. The otherworldiness of the local church must not be forgotten as it develops its plan of action for missions. Nor can it judge results as the world judges. Bottom-line figures are obvious and often helpful, but in the world of missions they never tell the whole story.

No effort in Jesus' name is ever lost. Too often in this world our efforts seem to go for naught. The famous South American hero Simon Bolivar is said to have lamented at the end of his life, "I have plowed in the sea." But in Christ each Christian is assured that the "Word [of God] does not . . . return void" (Isa. 55:11). The deed is never lost. Eternity preserves every effort in His name.

Above all, a plan of action must result in action. A fellowship should not be afraid to try even the boldest things or the smallest things in the name of Christ. Even as the meager resources of the little boy's lunch became the miracle that fed thousands, so what might seem to be meager efforts by a small fellowship might accomplish more than they ever thought or dreamed. Some of the great ministries of the world have developed from people who never thought that what they set out to do would have such far-reaching ramifications.

Persistance and Patience

A key aspect of the mission task of a local church is persistence and patience. The scriptural admonition to be patient in well-doing is perhaps the first truth believers in a local church caught up in the mission task must embrace. A local church may be locked into a ministry to an ethnic group that is highly resistant to its efforts. If it goes off licking its wounds and feeling unwanted and resented, it may stop just short of that point at which distrust gives way to trust and hostility gives way to openness and even appreciation. Adoniram Judson labored for ten years in the ancient kingdom of Burma before he recorded his first convert. Before that time he was rejected in hundreds of ways. He was imprisoned and was sick and all but despaired. Yet he persisted, and the people finally realized that his persistence was a witness to his convictions and to his credibility.[5]

Missions is not unlike farming. The ground has to be prepared, the seed has to be sowed, the emerging crop has to be tilled, and finally, it has to be harvested. Each phase is important, and nothing can be rushed. This is true in mission action. A local church has to be willing to persist in patience and wait on the harvest of its efforts.

Leadership and Prayer

Christ is the key to the mission of the local church. Christ's ongoing life in the church's midst through the indwelling Spirit and through Christ's example is the key. Humanly speaking, however, those people whom God has raised up in the midst of a local fellowship and endowed with the ability to guide and direct that fellowship are the keys to the church discovering its mission.

In the average church this responsibility falls on the pastor. Pastors may have all they can say grace over with ministry to the congregation. And yet, if the pastor does not lead the congregation to a sense of mission, and all that needs to follow, the church may lag in its growth because of this lack of vision. In many congregations, individual members have become the spark that heightens the awareness that begins the discovery of mission. But whether leadership begins with the pastor or among the people, the major need for a local church beginning to discover missions is to pray. Prayer provides the atmosphere of sensitivity in which God's leadership can emerge and the vision of mission can take place.

The vision that can come to a fellowship in an atmosphere of prayer can be transforming and contagious. R. Keith Parks, president of the Southern Baptist Convention's Foreign Mission Board, discussed God-given visions in a message to a group of supporters. He said that God-given visions

—begin with God,

—illuminate and enlighten past revelation,

—give understanding to a task to which people are sent, and

—begin to be embodied by even larger groups.[6]

But such visions emerge from a people in prayer. A local church seeking to discover its mission should begin on its knees.

Notes

1. John Berly, *An Outline of Missions* (Philadelphia: Muhlenberg Press, 1945), p. 60.

2. W. L. Howse and W. O. Thomason, *A Dynamic Church,* p. 74.

3. Baker J. Cauthen et als., *Advance: A History of Southern Baptist Foreign Mission.* Jesse C. Fletcher, "The Beginnings" p. 20.

4. Ibid. p. 8.

5. Courtney Anderson, *To the Golden Shore* (Boston: Little, Brown and Company, 1956).

6. Message to a group of financial backers in September of 1986 at Richmond, Virginia.

7

Mission in the Mean-time

Mission is in the mean-time. Mission is uniquely God's activity through the church in the mean-time, which is the time between the resurrection and the return of Christ. Oscar Cullman held that the missionary proclamation of the church, especially the preaching of the gospel, is what gives the time between the resurrection and second coming of Christ its connection with Christ's present dominion. Cullman believed that the coming of the kingdom depends not upon the result of this preaching but on the fact of it.[1]

In this regard Matthew 24:14 underlines two dramatic claims. First, the return of Christ waits on the preaching of the gospel to all nations. *The Living Bible* phrases that truth this way, "He is giving us time to get his message of salvation out to others" (2 Pet. 3:15). This is spelled out in the first line of the traditional Protestant missionary hymn, "O Zion, haste, thy mission high fullfilling." The time is critical for the church because no second chance is promised in the Scriptures. Men and women are to know the truth and have the opportunity to accept God's grace before the end.

Secondly, mission in itself hastens the Lord's coming. George E. Ladd said:

When we have accomplished our mission, He will return and establish His kingdom and glory. To us it is given not only to wait for but also to hasten the coming of the day of God.[2]

The thought that mission in itself is essential to the return of the Lord seems presumptuous, but it is clearly stated in Scripture.

What are we to do with these two compelling claims? More than one person has said, "If I really believed that, I could not sleep. I would have to exhaust myself going about telling every one of God's grace in Christ while there was still time. How do Christians believe such a thing and live their lives the way they do?"

In one sense such a remark is a stinging condemnation of Christian complacency in the face of their mission. It implies that Christians undermine what they say they believe when they do not exert every effort to fully carryout their mission day in and day out.

The thought that the timetables of God might rest on this process is very difficult to comprehend. Why would God wait on my procrastination, lack of courage, and perhaps even lack of conviction? One answer might be that God is patient with us and that judgment awaits not only those who have not accepted His grace but also those who have treated so lightly the responsibilities that come with it.

But the overall thrust of this statement is that mission in the mean-time is not something simply occupying the church between these two cosmic events on which human history seems to so directly turn. It is a part of the very meaning of the two events. Christ's resurrection and Christ's return anchor the mission of the church in a way that give cosmic meaning as well as urgency.

As George F. Vicedom pointed out, "In the new creation mission will no longer be necessary."[3] But in the mean-time, in the now, in our generation, in the place where each believer finds himself, mission is imperative.

A discussion of mission in the mean-time should not only look at the impact of the return of Christ on that mission but also look at the mean-time itself in terms of its nearness to the terminal point. It is not unlike a game in which the clock is running out and the whistle will soon blow. Mistakes become more critical, time is of the essence, a maximizing of final energies is required. What is the effect of end-time notions on mean-time mission? How do current dimensions of the mean-time both intimidate and encourage mission? What unique meaning do mean-time thoughts give to mission and to present-day believers sharply sensitive to that mission?

End-time and Mean-time

Beliefs about the end-time influence the way churches and Christians approach the task of mission.

No-Time Responses

Many Christians at different times in Christian history, but especially during the last two centuries, have felt that there was no time left. They have viewed biblical material that alludes to end-time, such as Matthew 24, as explaining the signs of their own times. Extremists have led believers to sell all that they owned in anticipation of the Lord's return on a certain date. Some have even climbed on their roofs to wait His coming. Any witness or mission in this context was hurried and incidental. Often there believers harshly judged other believers who felt there was still time to engage in the living of life and, especially, in witness to God's grace in Jesus Christ. Some books have fueled a more modern-day version of no-time responses.[4]

Since mission itself can be related to time, believers do well to remember Jesus' statement that no man knoweth when these last things will take place. (See Matt. 24:36.) No time responses appear to be wide of the mark biblically. Worse, they can leave those believers terribly disillusioned and all but ineffective if their speculation proves wrong.

Near-Time Responses

A less extreme response to biblical studies of last things is still fueled by the conviction that the end of time is drawing near. People who are convinced that Christ's return is approaching often bring a needed urgency to the task of personal witnessing and to the mission of the church. Such persons may become so intrigued with interpreting apocalyptic passages and studying the signs of the times that mission takes a backseat to the seemingly more exciting task of determining just how close Christ's return might be.

Such urgent strategies might also involve a reluctance to invest the time that mission requires to truly reach a people with the good news in Jesus Christ or make an impact on a particular need or in a particular area. Such near-time responses are often reluctant to use institutional approaches to the task, and, while institutions can obviously be overused in the mission of the church, they are often an accurate measure of the committment of a people to their mission.

Near-time responses can also involve a reluctance to enter into the church-planting strategies that have dominated missionary tactics over the years. The gathering of a church can be slow and tedious work, as people are led by the Spirit to become part of a congregation. The urgent need in a near-time frame of mind is simply to share the gospel with one person, urge him to do the same with another person and move on. On the other hand, if such persons are not gathered into local fellowships of believers as churches, their own lives are often stunted and their ability to function in the body of Christ greatly limited.

Near-time believers are often reluctant to consider nonwitness-type ministries. Addressing starvation or human suffering might seem irrelevant. Yet, clearly the mission of the church involves, if Christ's example prevails, a response to human suffering. And what about the Lord's desire to bring liberation to the oppressed? Christians have given lifetimes to such efforts. Would they be lost in near-time urgency?

Some-Time Responses

The next category is certainly not a synthesis to the first two nor enough of antithesis to the first to make the second a synthesis.[5] Some-time responses tend to lack a framework of urgency. These responses are fueled by the notion that while the clock might be ticking there is still plenty of time left. Some-time advocates feel that no-time responses and near-time responses come from literal readings of biblical materials that should be interpreted more symbolically and less urgently. Responses informed by a lack of urgency regarding the end-time might be patient, waiting for opportunities that need to be created by acting aggressively. Such responses might be directed toward long-time solutions, institutions, multigenerational plans and by being so patient run the risk of losing the original vision and ongoing urgency of mission.

Some-time responses may leave doubt that the mean-time is a linear process. They may see time more cyclically and God's requirements of us as more general than specific. Some-time responses may be like the ancients who, observing the winds, were reluctant to sow and, regarding the clouds, were reluctant to reap (see Eccl. 11:4). Obviously there should be an urgency in the concept of mission in the mean-time that is moving from resurrection toward the second coming.

True meaning for end-time implications and the mean-time of mission is found in the Lord's call to be found faithful. Monitoring the clock is not our task. On the football field the coach and the quarterback stay aware of the clock. The players are to play their hearts out right to the end without regard to the time remaining. The mean-time of mission is a time of urgency without holding one's spiritual breath. It is a time to be willing to plant trees that you might not sit under even as you harvest trees that you did not plant.[6]

During the student riots of the 1960s in France trees that were hundreds of years old were cut down by marauding students. One old Parisian is said to have remarked, "I am not so distressed about their cutting down trees as I am by the fact that they don't plant any."

The mean-time of missions calls not only for the urgency of cutting but also for the vision of planting. God takes care of the timing of the harvest.

Mean-time Intimidators

In the *meantime*, mission is, in the perspective of the average believer, in midstream. We are in the task with all of its fierceness and with all of its demands.

Opposition

Referring to this time, René Padilla said:

The period between the resurrection and the second coming is characterized by opposition to the Good News, opposition that is a foretaste of the final manifestation of the Anti-Christ. The opposition does not always come in terms of persecution. It also can take the form of seduction.[7]

Such opposition, whether it be persecution or seduction can be very intimidating to believers and to churches intent on mission.

Persectuion and Opposition

Persecution abounds in a global overview despite the fact that a great many Christians, such as those in the United States, enjoy complete tolerance, freedom to worship, and even cultural support for what they do. Christians who benefit from such conditions must not lose sight of the plight of their brothers and sisters in other parts of the world. Many of these suffer persecution of body and spirit for the cause of Jesus Christ.

Believers in China are again in contact with Christians of other lands. Visitors are allowed in that great country that was closed for so long under one Communist regime. Many Chinese Christians tell vivid stories of persecution during the Cultural Revolution that was led by the Red Guards. Believers evidently suffered horribly at the hands of Communists. Many Christians in other countries were totally unaware of their sufferings. Considering our oneness in Christ, that ought not to be.

Believers in some of the more evangelical and independent sects in the Soviet Union are presently under severe restrictions and often suffer persecution for their beliefs. Political camps and mental institutions become places of incarceration for believers who are too independent in their faith or too outspoken in proclaiming the gospel.

In some totalitarian countries in Latin America, believers intent on living out Christ's life in resisting evil, whether individually or state sponsored, have come under great persecution.

That is one of the reasons René Padilla and other theologians from the Third World often referred to the state as a form of the Antichrist.

The last few years provide eloquent illustrations in our own historical context of the way in which the state sets itself up as God and enslaves its citizens without the respect for the most basic human rights. Political murders, torture, disappearances, imprisonment without trial, concentrations camps—all this in the name of national security—are also signs of the Anti-Christ in Latin America.[8]

Many believers, Catholic and Protestant, have been caught up in such horrors in an effort to live out the mission of Jesus Christ. In their experience they have been, above all, brothers and sisters in Christ.

Padilla believed that the purpose of end-time reflections is not to invite us to discern the nature of the time but to be faithful to Jesus Christ in the life and mission of the present situation.

Lesslie Newbigin wrote: "The last and greatest efforts of the powers of this world must be to organize human history as a whole apart from obedience to Christ, that is to say in terms of the reign of Anti-Christ.[9] The original coming of Christ released the powers of evil against His life and His redemptive work in our behalf. The result was not only the crucifixion of the King of glory but also a reality that the mission of the church would have to contend with through the years.

Obviously there are many kinds of persecution. Some Christians have experienced theirs in the form of social ostracizing and cultural disapproval. To sustain mission without support is difficult at best, and it is one reason mission is best carried on from the base of a strong church aware of its task and with connectional relations with other equally committed Christians.

Numbers

One of the most seductive and intimidating factors in the mission of the church is the influence of the numbers involved. New global awareness, communication, and the ability to handle large masses of data make Christians more aware than ever of their numbers in relationship to the numbers of those who do not believe and even those who actively oppose them. In many countries in the world, the number of believers would be 1 percent or less of the population. In some of these countries, such as Japan, this number has prevailed over a long period of time, indicating little or no progress. Such realities can intimidate the church in its mission. The studies of urban growth and the number of Christians in urban centers are also intimidating. Christians must face the fact they are losing ground rapidly in the urban centers of the world.

Recent studies by Texas Baptists indicate that, despite their power and influence in that state, their growth in relation to the growth of Texas shows that they are losing ground steadily. The reason is that the population of Texas is exploding with an influx of people from other states and from Mexico. Their all-out efforts to establish new churches is an effort to counteract that reality. Such efforts reflect the intimidation of the numbers, but they also reflect a determination to do something about it.

Competition

Christians live in a pluralistic world. Ancient religions, such as Buddhism and Hinduism and Confucianism, have neither gone away nor lost their hold on large groups of people. The more aggressive Islam continues to be actively threatening and violent in its opposition to Christianity. New religious groups in Africa and the Orient, as well as Western versions of Eastern religions, reflect the continuing power of religion in the lives of people. Such pluralism offers strong competition to the gospel of Jesus Christ and evidence of needs that only Christ can truly meet.

Divisions

Christians have often felt their biggest problems came not so much from without as from within. Their own divisions and their inclination to oppose and even denounce each other over points that, from a historical perspective, may seem minor or even irrelevant. The ecumenical movement of the early 1900s that brought such organizations as the International Missionary Conference and the World Council of Churches into being was an effort to deal with the devastation of such divisions in the mission task. But even as Christians look for ways to relate to each other that recognize the variety of convictions and differences honestly held, divisions continue to wreck fellowships and dilute mission energies and weaken mission structures.

Doubts

A continuing intimidator of Christian mission comes from the doubts that are sown by Christians unable to assimilate either their own experiences or the new information being trumpeted around them. Their doubts may have followed opposition that turned them from the task or disappointments during times of unrealistic and even unbiblical expectations. They may have come from disillusionment caused by strong convictions not realized or clearly exposed as false. And, perhaps more than from anywhere else, doubt has come from the developing body of scientific knowledge that challenges old concepts about the age of the earth, the creation of man, the nature of the universe, and dimensions of what has heretofore been accorded the spiritual world. All of this intimidates missions in the mean-time.

Mean-time Encouragement

Since the resurrection of Jesus Christ, and especially since the launching of the Christian mission at Pentecost, believers have had to face intimidating factors. But there has always been encouragement. The Spirit is the primary source of encouragement. In this current mean-time, the church on mission has many sources of encouragement.

Infrastructure in Place

One reason many missiologists are greatly encouraged in this mean-time of mission is that there is a large framework for mission in place throughout the world. This framework of the church includes the institutions, societies, boards, agencies, cooperative relations, and vast connectional relationships already engaged in the task of mission. Some are broad-based structures, such as the Division of Missions of the Methodist Church, or the Foreign Mission Board of the Southern Baptist Convention, and others are highly specialized, such as the Wycliffe Translators, the Missionary Aviation Fellowship or the Far Eastern Broadcasting. Literally hundreds of such structures are engaged in some aspect of mission. Relief agencies, world hunger organizations, Christian medical societies, and educational programs of many kinds are at work. The Lausanne Conference of 1974, and the follow-up conferences, was a very important new sign of cooperation.[10]

Dialogues between various Christian groups, such as those between the Baptist World Alliance and the Lutheran World Body and between Protestant groups and the Roman church, can be helpful to the mission. Global consultations between representatives of the larger mission groups are being called with increasing regularity. New agencies have come into being specifically to share expertise from structure to structure.

Concentration and Communication

One reason this framework is so effective, or perhaps that it even exists, is the concentration of people that exists in this period of the mean-time. The great urban centers provide not only major challenges but also great opportunities. Large concentrations of people can be reached quickly with the same energies that in days gone by have been addressed to much smaller pockets of people and have required a much longer period of time. Radio and television, newspapers and magazines, telephones, satellite hookups, and computer networking mean new ways to reach people. Can the concentration and communication in place in our time be a new fullness? The church has a unique opportunity at this point in the mean-time.

Relevance of Message

Many secularists would attempt to dismiss the Christian message as outdated superstition, irrelevant to the post-atomic era and the space age. But many people believe that the message has never been more relevant.

As populations grow and concentrations of people expand, problems multiply. Managing the task of living with one another in a way that provides opportunity, security, and freedom for all is increasingly complex The gospel message speaks to these problems as no other message does. The new work that Christ accomplishes in an individual relates that individual to others in a way that alone can accomplish true community. While the Bible does not promise on this earth a perfect society, seeking individuals find in the good news of the kingdom of God the answer to the deepest yearnings of their hearts.

With the shadow of a nuclear holocaust hovering over civilization, the concept of a transcending reality and encompassing eternity gives an important dimension to the struggle. While some Christians use it as an argument to passively accept such threats of disaster, others see it as new encouragement to bring the mission of the church to a world struggling with its life as a global village. With people suddenly aware of how crowded planet Earth really is and how difficult it is to meet the common needs of so diverse a people suddenly placed in each others backyards, the church's mission looms more relevant than ever.

Current Victories

One of the most encouraging dimensions of the mean-time is a growing list of contemporary victories. These victories include such things as the rapid evangelization of the Giryama Tribe in East Africa, Pentecostal gains in northern Latin America, resurgence of free church Christianity in the Soviet Union, and the remarkable survival of the church in China during such a long period of persecution. New dialogues between Christians seeking the singular message that is their common property can only help Christians and churches in their task.

There is a tremendous temptation to list victories reported by mission boards and agencies and even individual church groups caught up in the mission throughout the world. Many feel the fastest growing Christian arena may be in developing nations.

Revival Potential

While the word sounds out of place today, *revival* best describes the wildfire potential in the church's carrying out its mission. A recent report from Tanzania's Kyela district revealed over fourteen hundred baptisms in a single year from the work of two agricultural missionaries and eight African evangelists. Over half of these converts were turned over to other denominational groups. For nine years the district experienced a 59 percent average annual growth in baptisms.[11]

Throughout its history, the gospel has found the susceptibility of great need and great opportunity and spread from person to person and house to house like the good news that it is. This potential gives an excitement to the mission of the church that is hard to describe. It cannot be contained, nor can it be put on a trend line since explosive dimensions are inherent in what it does.

In the Mean-time

Mission in the mean-time is the mission of the church now. There is an unquestioned urgency about it, and there is a commitment to it as never before. Due to the nature of the darkness into which the light has come, persecution and opposition have not ceased; nor is there any likelihood they will. The task is still awesome, and secular advances have undermined most of the culturally supported bases that the churches have enjoyed in past years. Time might reveal, however, that the power of the mission functions best without such support.

Notes

1. Ralph Winter, *Perspectives On the World Christian Movement: A Reader,* George E. Ladd, *Perspectives on the World Christian Movement: A Reader* (Pasadena, Calif: William Carey Library, 1981), p.69.

2. Ibid., p. 69.

3. George F. Vicedom, *The Message of God* (St. Louis, Mo.: Concordia Publishing House, 1965) p. 142.

4. Hal Lindsey, *The Late Great Planet Earth* (Grand Rapids, Mich.: Zondervan Publishing House, 1970).

5. Referring to the dialectic concept of thesis, antithesis, and synthesis.

6. Gordon Clinard, *Planting Trees You Will Never Sit Under* (Abilene, Tex.: Hardin-Simmons University, 1977).

7. C. René Padilla, *Mission Between Times* (Grand Rapids, Mich.: William B. Eerdmans Publishing Company, 1985), p.123.

8. Ibid, p. 125.

9. Lesslie Newbigin, *A Faith for This One World?* (New York: Harper & Brothers, 1961), pp. 112-113.

10. International Congress on World Evangelization was held in Lausanne, Switzerland, July 16-25, 1974. It included 2,473 participants from 150 churches in 153 Protestant denominations.

11. Robert O'Brien, Foreign Mission Board News Service, as reported in the *Baptist Standard,* October 15, 1986.

Conclusion

How does one write a conclusion about a subject that is still very much in motion? Because mission is in the meantime and because the church is yet in the middle of her task, the mission of the church is by definition incomplete. Perhaps summary of what is obviously a bare-bones overview of the task of the church is as much as can be attempted.

The mission of the church is at the heart of the church's reason for being. Understanding that the church is the result of God's mission and that in Christ it becomes the church's mission is the beginning point. The Bible defines the mission and contains the church's marching orders. The march of mission provides one way to understand the church's position now. Understanding the kaleidoscopic dimensions of its message over the ages may be another.

Believers must ultimately translate the mission of the church into the task of a local church. Mission in the meantime sets the task firmly in the here and now.

But inherent in the foregoing is the feeling that mission is still in transition and once more at a crossroads. Consideration of the nature of this transition and the shape of these crossroads can inform and direct mission-minded believers and churches.

Mission in Transition

The chapter on the march of mission and the one on the message of mission illustrate that mission is always in transition. However, there are certain obvious transitions in progress.

Sectarian to Church

Mission is in transition from sectarian dimensions to church dimensions. Through the years the church has splintered into a multitude of sectarian compartments as it attempted to define and protect precious notions and especially as it broke away from state domination and from ecclesiastical oppression. The recovery of the Bible for the average believer accelerated the process.

The great expansion in missions in the nineteeth century provoked ecumenical thoughts as a heightened sense of mission began to nudge the church from sectarian to church perspectives. Ecumenism brought its own strife and division. Recently a new form of ecumenism has emerged from evangelical Christianity rather than from liturgical Christianity. The movement from sectarian to church is much different than from denomination to ecumenism. It is less organization and more perception. Whether this trend from sectarian to church will be successful remains to be seen, but the fact is that mission is in transition from a sectarian to church perception of its task.

Parochial to Global

Mission is also in transition from parochial to global dimensions. While citing how important it is to see the mission of the church in the context of a local church, the church's problem through the years has often been just the opposite (that is, the inability to see it beyond narrow perspectives).

Only in recent years have Christians begun to envision the mission task as global. As we are able through the magic of space travel and television to look back on our own globe spinning in the sky as a part of something immensely bigger, there is no way that the mission task can be considered anything but global. Indeed, the day may come where it has to be considered global in the broadest sense of that word.

Rural to Urban

Mission is also in transition from rural to urban. The data being developed by David B. Barrett shows just how rapidly the world's populations are concentrating in giant cities and what new challenges this presents to the missionary task. In the Western world, for instance, the church often lodged its most solid roots in rural environments. Indeed, many of the people who have scattered around the world under a personal missionary mandate have come from such dedicated fellowships of believers. But the developing urban world demands new skills from mission forces and from the church committed to mission. Churches will find more and more opportunities at their doorsteps, as well as more challenges to be a part of connectional efforts to reach cities beyond itself.

Narrow to Holistic

Mission is in transition too from the narrow to the holistic in its scope. One of the things that the march of mission revealed, and the message of mission underscored, was the fact that the task often has been interpreted too narrowly. At times it was simply the claims of the church, a kind of ecclesiastical interpretation; at other times it was more narrowly construed in terms of a person's soul with the total lack of concern for his whole life. At other times it was carried out in purely humanistic terms as if it had no spiritual dimension. At times mission has been more of an accultura-tion process, a kind of civilizing effort in terms of whatever base the missioner came from. But increasingly mission is being interpreted in holistic terms, reaching out to all human needs just as Jesus Christ did. Since we are sent as He was sent, He is still our model for mission.

Mission is in transition from a facet of the church's life to the whole of its life. Often mission has been interpreted as the other part of the church's task along with worship, teaching, and pastoral care and ministry. Now it is being understood at the heart of the church's life, even as expressed in worship. It is the basic assumption of all that is taught. It is at the heart of pastoral care and all ministries.

The Church at Crossroads

The march of mission reveals that the church has been at a crossroads many times. The crossroads we face now are probably not the last crossroads the church will confront. But some obvious crossroads are before the church in its mission.

Secularism

Few people would doubt that the barnacles of secularism have attached themselves to the hull of the church's ship. This has been true from the beginning, but it is certainly a recognized reality now. A church discovers that it does busi-ness like the world, that it communicates like the world, that its message is often a thinly disguised rehash of the world's message, and that it even relates to the world according to worldly wisdom and not spiritual wisdom. It will rationalize this by pointing out that it has influenced the world to the point to where you can't tell which is the chicken and which is the egg. But the fact is that many secular dimensions (barnacles) inhibit the progress of the church's response to

Jesus' commands, and they need to be scraped free. The church is at a crossroads primarily because it is beginning to recognize those barnacles and to want a cleaner hull.

Body Life

The church is at a crossroads because it is ready to sense the relationship of the spiritual body and a spiritual head. Body concepts of church promote the importance of every individual and an awareness of the headship of Christ in ordering the activities of the individual believers that make up a local church. New appreciation for one another will bring many more people into the task of missions. A new sensitivity of the headship of Jesus Christ will empower these tasks as they have never been empowered before.

This particular perception brings about a lot of shaking of the foundations. The way the church understands its clergy and laity, the way the church views its authoritative structures, and the way the church understands the leadership of Christ all make an impact on the church's mission. To those who insist upon a strictly biblical interpretation of Christ's leadership, those who are highly subjective and sensitive to the indwelling Spirit will constitute a threat. The former challenges the orthodoxy of the latter while the latter dismiss the former as legalists and quenchers of the Spirit. The church is at a crossroads as it tries to sense how as the body of Christ it should understand itself and respond to His headship through the indwelling Spirit.

Trivia and Trials

And finally, the church is at a crossroads in its efforts to transcend both the trivia that besets it and the trials that threaten it. The trivia includes traditions that have become more important in themselves than in what they say and whom they honor. The trivia can emerge from tasks that keep members of the church busy but do not bear on the mission of the church. Trivia can come from a preoccupation with the maintenance of the fellowship itself rather than the fellowship's preoccupation with the task. Church disputes simply evaporate when the church unites around a demanding task that is at the heart of its reason for being.

But the church is not without trials at this crossroads either. Those trials come from an increasingly assertive secularism, an environment often hostile to the Christian faith, and competition from traditional religious expressions as well as emerging ones.

God's Conclusion

A friend of mine often enjoys exhorting any congregation to which he is ministering to turn to the back of the Bible, to the closing Book of Revelation for instruction on what to expect in the future. He says, "Look in the back of the book if you want to find the answers. You will find that God wins."

One thing the church in mission must keep in mind is that it is God's battle and God has already revealed His victory. The church is not in the task on its own, nor has God cut it loose to sink or swim. It is an extension of His continued mission in Jesus Christ. The church is vital to the full realization of the kingdom, and it is in a no-lose situation. The fact that the larger church can at any given point in time, or a local church can in any place in time, fail to participate and realize the excitement and joy of being a part of what God is doing does not take away the reality of God's victory.

One of the exciting things about the mission of the church is that it tackles doubts and the fear of the future head-on. What might go wrong is incidental because God buys up our defeats and makes victories out of them. He takes our mistakes and converts them into new opportunities. It is God's work. God calls us to it. God blesses us in it.

The mission of the church is bigger than any believer. Yet in the midst of it, every believer is bigger than he ever thought he could be. The task by itself looks too big, but a great God cuts it down to every believer's size. The key is to see that in Christ, each of us, every day, and all the world is inextricably involved in that mission.

Bibliography

Aberly, John. *An Outline of Missions.* Philadelphia: Muhlenberg Press, 1945.

Amberson, Talmadge R., comp. *The Birth of Churches.* Nashville: Broadman Press, 1979.

Anderson, Gerald H. *Christian Mission in Theological Perspective.* Nashville: Abingdon Press, 1967.

Anderson, Gerald H. *The Theology of the Christian Mission.* New York: McGraw Hill Book Co., Inc, 1961.

Anderson, William K. *Christian World Mission.* Nashville: Parthenon Press, 1946.

Austin, Bill. *Austin's Topical History of Christianity.* Wheaton: Tyndale House Publishers, Inc., 1983.

Barrett, David B. *World-Class Cities & World Evangelization.* Birmingham: New Hope Press, 1986.

Belew, M. Wendell. *Churches and How They Grow.* Nashville: Broadman Press, 1983.

Blauw, Johannes. *The Missionary Nature of the Church.* New York: McGraw-Hill Book Co., 1962.

Brunner, Emil. *The Word in the World.* London: CSM Press, 1931.

Buttrick, George Arthur. *The Interpreters Bible,* vol. 7. Nashville: Abingdon Press, 1951.

Carver, William O. *Missions in the Plan of the Ages.* Chicago: Fleming H. Revell Co., 1909; Nashville: Broadman Press, 1951.

_____. *The Course of Christian Missions* Chicago: Fleming H. Revell Co., 1932.

Cauthen, Baker J. et als. *Advance: A History of Southern Baptist Foreign Missions.* Nashville: Broadman Press, 1970.

Copeland, E. Luther. *World Mission and World Survival.* Nashville: Broadman Press, 1985.

Crawley, Winston. *Global Mission: A Story to Tell.* Nashville: Broadman Press, 1985.

Deane, William F. *Third World Liberation Theologies.* Maryknoll: Orbis Books, 1986.

DuBose, Francis M. *Classics of Christian Missions.* Nashville: Broadman Press, 1979.

_____. *God Who Sends.* Nashville: Broadman Press, 1983.

Glasser, Arthur F. and Donald A. McGavran. *Contemporary Theologies of Mission.* Grand Rapids: Baker Book House, 1983.

Goerner, H. Cornell. *All Nations in God's Purpose.* Nashville: Broadman Press, 1979.

Howse, W. L. and W. O. Thomason. *A Dynamic Church: Spirit and Structure for the 70's.* Nashville: Convention Press, 1969.

Horner, Norman A. *Protestant Crossroads in Mission.* Nashville: Abingdon Press, 1968.

Johnson, Clyde M. *The Trouble in Our Church.* Houston: D. Armstrong Co., 1981.

Kane, J. Herbert. *A Global View of Christian Missions,* rev. ed. Grand Rapids: Baker Book House, 1971.

Kane, J. Herbert. *Understanding Christian Missions.* Grand Rapids: Baker Book House, 1972.

_____. *Understanding Christian Missions Third Addition.* Grand Rapids: Baker Book House, 1982.

Latourette, Kenneth Scott. *A History of Christianity.* New York: Harper & Row, 1953.

McClellan, Albert. *The Missions Tasks of a Church.* Nashville: Convention Press, 1969.

McGavran, Donald Anderson. *The Bridge of God.* New York: Friendship Press, 1981.

McGraw, Larry R. An Examination of the Literacy Context of the Great Commission in Matthew 28:16-20, Ph.D. dissertation from Southwestern Baptist Theological Seminary, 1983.

Mawry, Charles E. *The Church and the New Generation.* Nashville: Abingdon, 1968 © 1969.

Newman, Albert Henry. *A Manual of Church History.* Philadelphia: The American Baptist Publishing Society, 1899; rev. 1933, 1951.

O'Brien, Bill. *Mission for Tomorrow.* Nashville: Broadman Press, 1980.

Peters, George W. *A Biblical Theology of Missions.* Chicago: Moody Press, 1971.

Simmons Robert A. *O Church Awake.* North Quincy: Christopher Publishing, 1969.

Stott, John R. W. *Christian Mission in the Modern World.* Downers Grove: Inter-Varsity Press, 1975.

Vicedom, George F. *The Mission of God.* St. Louis: Concordia Publishing House, 1965.

Vos, Howard F. *Beginnings in Church History.* Chicago: The Moody Institute, 1977.

Wagner, C. Peter. *On the Crest of the Wave.* Ventura: Regal Books, 1983.

Walker, Arthur L., Jr. *Educating for Christian Missions: Supporting Christian Missions Through Education.* Nashville: Broadman Press, 1981.

Willis, Avery, Jr. *Biblical Basis of Missions.* Nashville: Convention Press, 1979.

Winter, Ralph D. ed., *Perspective on the World Christian Movement: A Reader.* Pasadena: William Carey Library, 1981.

Index